2012 Asian Pacific Americans Corporate Survey

Measuring the Positive Effect of Diversity

Thank you to all our supporters:

PLATINUM   **GOLD**

TimeWarner

SILVER

 CORNING Goldman Sachs

BRONZE

BNY Mellon, Colgate-Palmolive Company, GE, KPMG LLP, Marsh & McClennan, McDonald's, Merck, National Grid, New York Life Insurance Company, Pfizer

Special thanks to those who helped support and guide this survey and report to completion:

SENIOR ADVISOR

Philip A. Berry, President, Philip Berry Associates LLC
Author: *Being Better Than You Believe: 8 Steps to Ultimate Success*

SURVEY STEERING COMMITTEE

Maurice Cox, Former Vice President, Corporate Development & Diversity, PepsiCo

Neddy Perez, Vice President, Diversity & Inclusion, Ingersoll Rand

Aida Sabo, Vice President, Diversity and Inclusion, Cardinal Health

Amy Shang, Managing Director, HSBC

Todd Sears, Founder, Coda, LLC

Deborah Turner Bailey, Global Diversity Officer, Human Resource Director, Corning Incorporated

SURVEY PRODUCTION TEAM

David Whitelaw Reid, Director of Corporate Relations, Asia Society

Michael G. Kulma, Executive Director, Global Leadership Initiatives, Asia Society

Jonathan Saw, Project Manager, Asian Pacific Americans Corporate Survey, Asia Society

Asia Society Global Talent and Diversity Council

AS OF APRIL 30, 2012

Purpose of the Council: To advise Asia Society on how best to leverage its public voice in the area of global talent and diversity leadership and how to best serve Corporate Members with their global leadership objectives. The Council provides a regular forum for members to share best practices on the leadership challenges they face in the U.S. and Asia.

CO-CHAIRS

Ron Glover
VP, Diversity and Workforce Policy
IBM

Stephanie N. Mehta
Executive Editor
Fortune Magazine

Nereida Perez
VP, Diversity & Inclusion
Ingersoll Rand

MEMBERS

Rohini Anand
SVP & Global Chief Diversity Officer
Sodexo

Letty Ashworth
General Manager Global Diversity
Delta Air Lines, Inc.

Anthony Carter
VP, Global Diversity & Inclusion
Chief Diversity Officer
Johnson & Johnson

Jyoti Chopra
Managing Director
Global Communications
Deloitte Touche Tohmatsu Limited

Deborah Dagit
Chief Diversity Officer
Merck & Co.

Manolet G. Dayrit
Partner
KPMG LLP

Ana Duarte-McCarthy
Chief Diversity Officer
Citigroup

Deborah Elam
Chief Diversity Officer
GE

Edward Gadsden
SVP & Chief Diversity Officer
Pfizer Inc.

Michelle Gadsden-Williams
Managing Director, Global Head
of Diversity & Inclusion
Credit Suisse

Apoorva Gandhi
VP, Multicultural Markets & Alliances
Marriott International

Aynesh Johnson
VP, Global Leadership & Diversity
Goldman, Sachs & Co.

Donna Johnson
Chief Diversity Officer
MasterCard Worldwide

Eugene Kelly
Worldwide Director
Global Diversity & Inclusion
Colgate-Palmolive Company

Kathryn Komsa
VP, Diversity & Inclusion
Marsh & McLennan Companies, Inc.

Denice Kronau
Chief Diversity Officer
Siemens

Lisa Mink
Executive Director
Global Diversity and Inclusion
Dell

Joanne Rodgers
VP & Chief Diversity Officer
New York Life Insurance Company

Aida Sabo
VP, Diversity & Inclusion
Cardinal Health

Amy Shang
Managing Director
HSBC

Jeffrey Siminoff
Managing Director
Head of Global Inclusion
Morgan Stanley

Marva Smalls
EVP, Global Inclusion Strategy
Viacom

Barbara Stern
Director of Global Personnel
& Talent Management
McKinsey & Company

Geri Thomas
SVP, Global Diversity & Inclusion
Executive and Georgia Market President
Bank of America

Debra Turner Bailey
Global Diversity Officer
& Human Resource Director
Corning Incorporated

Ali Walji
VP & Diversity Officer
Chartls

Sheena Wilson
Global Head of Talent Strategy
BNY Mellon

Melinda Wolfe
Head of Professional Development
Bloomberg

ADVISORS

Vishakha N. Desai
President
Asia Society

Subha Barry*

Philip A. Berry*
President
Philip Berry Assoc. LLC

Michael E. Chen

Maurice Cox

Ted Childs
Principal
Ted Childs LLC

Geraldine Gallashaw

J.D. Hokoyama

Lance A. LaVergne

Todd Sears
Founder
Coda LLC

*Indicates Founding Co-Chairs

Table of Contents

Introduction

It is hard to believe that when the Asia Society first developed the Asian Pacific Americans Corporate Survey in 2010, there was little data about Asian Pacific American (APA) employees beyond the number of APAs employed in the United States. While there is still a long way to go, with the guidance of our Global Talent and Diversity Council, we have been able to expand knowledge about APA employees and provide guidance on how best to address their needs, concerns and aspirations.

What has become apparent is that to get diversity "right" the overall discussion must be expanded to include Asia Pacific Americans. Their supposed success is belied by the lack of APA representation at the very top of most companies. In addition, the overall "positive" APA stereotype in the workplace demonstrates that the issue is less one of skills acquisition than of perceptions and differences in treatment. The need to add the missing APA piece of the diversity puzzle is apparent to most companies at the Fortune 500 level, like those in our survey. This year's findings provide even more fodder on how companies should move forward.

In 2012, we looked deeper into the critical factor of Time in the U.S. and discovered that its impact was more than a simple matter of longevity in the United States. We asked respondents who were not born in the U.S. to tell us at what age they arrived. Those who came as children (10 years old or younger) had perceptions of their companies that were largely identical to APAs who were born in the U.S. This more clearly indicates, as we suggested in 2011, that these perceptions are linked to having an American identity and the resultant higher expectations of companies.

This concept of identity is illustrated in the experience of many first-generation APA families. The parents in the family often use the word "American" to describe anyone non-Asian and often as a synonym for "Caucasian." The vocabulary distinction reflects an internal distinction they make between themselves and their adopted country. At the same time, their children are more apt to use "American" to describe themselves, regardless of whether they were born on U.S. soil or came here as small children.

From a practical perspective for companies, this reinforces the need to expand the prism through which their APA employees are viewed, and take into account other factors beyond country of origin. In fact, the 2012 survey data again shows that country of origin differences are largely explained by demographic differences. Thus it is less important to understand whether APA employees are Chinese, Indian, Korean, Japanese or Filipino and more important to have programs that can address an array of individual circumstances.

The importance of long-term maintenance and support of such programs is exemplified by this year's Best in Class companies. While budgets for training and development programs are often the first to be reduced or cut entirely in economic downturns, maintaining that investment has real effects for employees. For example, despite the overall decrease in favorability scores, employees at Best in Class companies maintain overall positive favorability on the Professional Growth and Development dimension (54 percent). Other companies, meanwhile, saw favorability scores fall from an already low 45 percent to just 35 percent this year.

We continued the effort to uncover and highlight Best Practices in APA employee engagement in 2012 as well. Mentoring and sponsorship examples were added, as these are widely recognized as being integral to the development and career success of all employees, not just those who are APAs. Regardless of dimension, the Best Practices indicate that at times, success is not dependent on having an APA-specific program, but rather on having an overall strategic and integrated approach that could have synergies with other groups or for the company culture as a whole.

Finally, we undertook a further analysis of the engagement drivers in this year's survey. In addition to identifying what they are, we looked at the intersection of each dimension and how it drove overall employee satisfaction. In short, we found that diversity works and has a measurable effect on APA employee satisfaction.

—VISHAKHA N. DESAI, PRESIDENT, ASIA SOCIETY

Background
and Methodology

Background and Methodology

Asia Society first conducted the Asian Pacific Americans Corporate Survey in 2010. It is the first survey that exclusively measures and recognizes policies and practices that professionally develop Asian Pacific Americans (APAs) working at Fortune 500 and similar companies. The survey's purpose is to provide both quantitative and qualitative information regarding APA employees.

Asia Society partnered with Proximo Consulting, a third-party survey vendor, to facilitate a two-part evaluation process. In one part, a targeted employee survey provided APA employees with an opportunity to share their experiences regarding their company's success in developing and promoting their careers, and supporting APA culture and community.

Simultaneously, corporate diversity officers and human resource executives from each participating company described the programs, policies and activities that support APA employees. The Asian Pacific Americans Corporate Survey is the only survey that compares responses from both groups.

The 2012 survey, which was conducted between November 1, 2011 and February 24, 2012, represents the opinions, insights and experiences of close to 2,000 APA employees. Respondents represent the full range of professional levels and business/industry types across the United States. The survey measures key workplace and career dimensions that impact today's APA employees. The six dimensions are defined as follows:

- ▶ **Diversity:** General workplace culture, and commitment to diversity and representation
- ▶ **Professional Growth and Development:** Opportunities for growth and development, mentoring, and role models
- ▶ **Commitment to the APA Community Internally and Externally:** Relationships with the APA community, support for APA Employee Resource Groups and relevance of company activities within the APA community
- ▶ **Leadership and Company Image:** Employee impressions of company efforts directed toward understanding the APA and Asian markets, and drawing upon the experiences and expertise of its APA employees to inform customer engagement in the markets
- ▶ **The Job Itself:** Employee perceptions about fulfilling their potential, and being valued for their strengths and skills at their company
- ▶ **Satisfaction, Commitment and Belonging:** Measures of satisfaction, commitment to the company and feelings of belonging

Further insights are drawn from employee responses by examining each dimension according to the following six demographics:

- ▶ Age
- ▶ Age of Arrival in the U.S. (for those not born in the U.S.)
- ▶ Executive Leadership Track and Job Level
- ▶ Gender
- ▶ Time in the U.S.
- ▶ Years with Current Employer

An analysis of survey results was also performed to determine individual engagement drivers that influence employee satisfaction and action steps that can help build higher satisfaction levels. In addition, the survey features a number of best practices focusing on real-life strategies for successfully attracting, developing and retaining APA leaders.

Executive Summary

The rising importance of Asian Pacific Americans in the United States, driven by their increasing population, wealth, confidence, and leadership, makes them a crucial demographic that cannot be ignored. This is particularly the case in Corporate America. While Asian Pacific Americans have made tremendous strides in the workplace, much work still needs to be done. The 2012 Asian Pacific Americans Corporate Survey shows that the lynchpin for APA employee engagement and satisfaction remains the Professional Growth and Development dimension. However, interlocking relationships between all the dimensions, as well as the complexities within the APA population itself, require a multi-faceted approach.

Key Findings

- **Companies need to do more to draw on the expertise and knowledge of their APA employees,** which represent untapped potential for companies as they seek to understand both the APA market and Asian markets. According to the 2010 U.S. Census the APA market has grown by 44 percent between 2000 and 2010. Well under half (41 percent) of APAs agree that their company draws on APA employees when engaging APA customers, with only a slightly higher percentage (42 percent) believing so when working with customers from Asia.

- **Growth and development can be addressed in many ways,** for example, through focusing on the dimensions of Commitment to the APA Community Internally and Externally and Leadership and Company Image. APA employees recognize and appreciate the support for employee resource groups. However, they indicate that activities with the larger APA community externally could be more business relevant, which would enable them to better put their skills and expertise to work.

- **Despite great loyalty, APA employees do not feel a sense of belonging at their companies.** This feeling of not belonging can be attributed to many concrete factors, such as the lack of APA role models and mentors, low APA representation in the company's leadership ranks, and feelings that companies do not value their skills and experience as Asian Pacific Americans in the context of conducting business.

- **The longer APAs are in the U.S. the greater the decline in positive responses across virtually every workplace dimension.** APAs who came here as children, and thus have more of an American identity, view their companies less favorably than those who came to the U.S. later in life.

- **There is a dynamic of decreasing engagement at the critical career juncture between middle and senior management.** Lack of professional growth opportunities leads to APA attrition, which exacerbates the lack of APA mentors and role models, leading to even less engagement. From 30 to 59 years old, most professionals make the transition from middle to senior management. This is also the time when the decline in APA employee job satisfaction begins to take hold.

- **Companies must ensure APA employees feel valued.** The focus of Best in Class companies on issues of mentoring and sponsorship highlights the connection between having these relationships and employee engagement.

Certain aspects of the 2012 findings merit a deeper dive as they further illuminate the matrix of needs, desires and engagement drivers at work within the APA employee population.

Implications of APAs' American Identity

The 2011 survey revealed that Time in the U.S. for APA employees is one of the most determinative demographics for their engagement and satisfaction. This year, not only is the finding still applicable, but an additional nuance has been added—Age of Arrival in the U.S.

Though not as consistent as the Time in the U.S. results, there is a similar decline in favorability, with those who arrived in the U.S. as children having favorability scores that were essentially the same as native-born APAs. They differed in statistically significant ways from those in the *"Teen"* or *"Adult"* groups, whose scores were broadly similar to each other.

Respondents who have been in the U.S. for similar periods of time exhibit differences in satisfaction according to the Age of Arrival. The decline in favorability is not a simple factor of longevity in this country.

APAs with a strong American identity share the same job and career expectations as their non-APA counterparts and are thus more aware of workplace inequities that ultimately impact them. The result is an overall erosion in the optimism and enthusiasm they had at the start of their career.

APAs with less time in the U.S., or who moved to the U.S. later in life, have higher satisfaction due to both different priorities and less awareness or focus on the inequities they encounter.

Need to Leverage APA Employees to Increase Company Understanding of the Asian and APA Consumer Markets

The 2012 survey further distinguished companies' efforts to better understand both APA and Asian consumer markets.

Within the survey's Leadership and Company Image dimension, APA employees indicate that there is a measurable difference between their company's understanding of the APA market and the Asian markets. Although a clear majority of APAs (61 percent) believe their senior executives understand Asian markets, only a slim majority (53 percent) credit their company's leadership with the same knowledge of the APA market.

These results indicate that companies can potentially increase their knowledge of and insights into the APA market by applying to it the same strategic efforts and focus that they bring to understanding the Asian markets. In the process, companies can not only expand their business in one of the world's most dynamic markets, but also make significant strides in taking advantage of the opportunities presented by the APA market itself.

It should be noted that in this area, differences in company focus are paramount. Participating companies range from those with extensive Asian operations to those that are almost exclusively domestically focused. However, for both types of companies, an internal strategy that includes more actively seeking the counsel of APA employees and promoting awareness of their expertise across leadership and management levels could be important employee engagement strategies. Survey results support the need for additional proactive efforts—only 41 to 42 percent of APA employees agree that their companies draw on their knowledge and experience to engage either market. This represents an untapped employee engagement opportunity.

Strategic Action Steps

The complex and closely connected interactions between all the dimensions studied in the survey, indicate that companies can focus their efforts on any one of them, in order to increase overall APA engagement and satisfaction. The salient question is thus: Which dimensions provide the most practical strategic action steps?

Following are action steps for a number of the dimensions under study. By breaking down these topline steps into ever more granular actions, companies can determine their unique path to addressing engagement and satisfaction of their APA employees.

Professional Growth and Development

Strategic Action Steps:

- ► Offer career growth and development opportunities to APA employees.

- ► Support APAs' participation in leadership skills-building activities.

- ► Create a clear presence of APA employees in senior leadership positions.

Commitment to APA Community Internally and Externally

Strategic Action Steps:

- ► Establish and maintain strong ties with the APA community.

- ► Support APA Employee Resource Groups.

- ► Offer business-relevant activities with the APA community, which extend beyond holiday and festival celebrations.

Leadership and Company Image

Strategic Action Steps:

- ► Build a positive image in the APA community.

- ► Ensure that company leaders understand the APA market.

- ► Ensure that company leaders understand Asian markets.

Dimension Analysis

Maintaining Overall Satisfaction Levels, Identifying Opportunities for Improvement

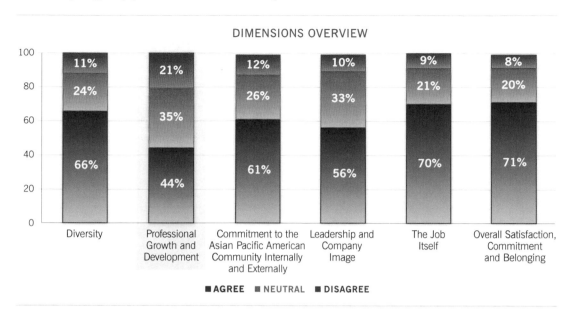

DIMENSIONS OVERVIEW

■ AGREE ■ NEUTRAL ■ DISAGREE

The 2012 survey findings remain fairly consistent with the 2011 data with scores on each dimension varying by one to three percentage points. The majority of APA employees—from a low of 56 percent to a high of 71 percent—continue to give high marks to each dimension. Professional Growth and Development remains the exception, with satisfaction dropping from 50 percent to 44 percent since 2011. This is probably due, in large part, to the effects of the softness in the overall economy, which affects all employees. However, it could indicate that APA employees may be feeling these effects more acutely.

Also as in years past, neutral responses are still a noticeably significant percentage of overall responses, ranging from 20 percent to 35 percent. The percentage of APA survey participants who are neutral on dimension topics either increased or remained unchanged. Professional Growth and Development also experienced the greatest rise in neutral responses—seven percent.

While these percentages are often interpreted to mean that APA employees are less likely to take a position, it is also likely that the *"neutral"* group represents an APA population that is influence-able and reserving judgment until they know more about their company's efforts relating to the dimensions studied.

> **The high proportion of neutral responses could represent a large influence-able APA employee population.**

Diversity:
APAs Seeking to Bring More of Their Talents to Their Companies

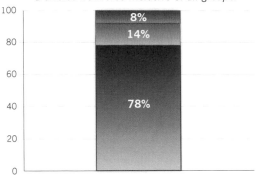

"My company's mission statement articulates a commitment to creating and maintaining a diverse workforce inclusive of all groups."

8%
14%
78%

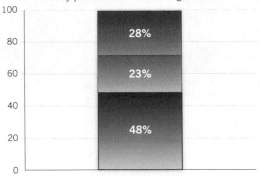

"This company has an ample representation of individuals with Asian Pacific American backgrounds in key positions within the organization."

28%
23%
48%

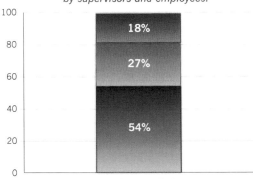

"This company's efforts to develop Asian Pacific Americans are fully supported by supervisors and employees."

18%
27%
54%

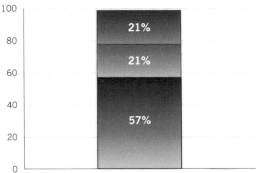

"Promotions are awarded to the most deserving employees, regardless of gender, ethnicity, etc."

21%
21%
57%

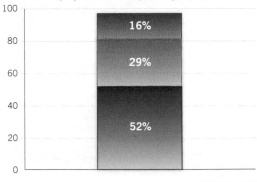

"In our work group, we capitalize on the perspectives and talents of Asian Pacific American employees in accomplishing objectives."

16%
29%
52%

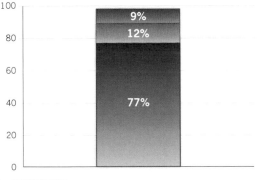

"I work in an environment that is free from disrespectful and offensive behavior toward Asian Pacific Americans."

9%
12%
77%

■ AGREE   ■ NEUTRAL   ■ DISAGREE

APA employees recognize the dramatic strides their companies have made in workplace diversity. The majority expressed their satisfaction with their company's success developing an all-inclusive mission statement (78 percent), creating and maintaining an environment that is respectful of APAs (77 percent), awarding promotions based solely on performance (57 percent) and launching internally supported efforts to develop APAs in the workplace (54 percent).

Although clear advances have been made in diversity, some concerns remain over the extent to which team members capitalize on APA contributions and APA leadership opportunities. These are the two lowest-scoring diversity areas.

Less than half of APAs (48 percent) believe their company has appointed APA professionals in key positions and only a slim majority (52 percent) agree that their team takes advantage of their perspectives and talents when achieving its goals.

APA employees do not feel their talents and contributions are fully recognized.

The common thread between these two findings is the perception by APA employees that their value and contributions are not being fully recognized, utilized or represented within the organization. Takeaway: By taking a wider view of APA employees' talents, expertise and perspectives; offering skills-building leadership training and profile-raising mentoring programs; and promoting accordingly, company leaders can significantly improve APA professional opportunities and engagement levels.

Professional Growth and Development:
Continued Challenges with Role Models and Senior Leadership Presence, Despite Recognition of Support

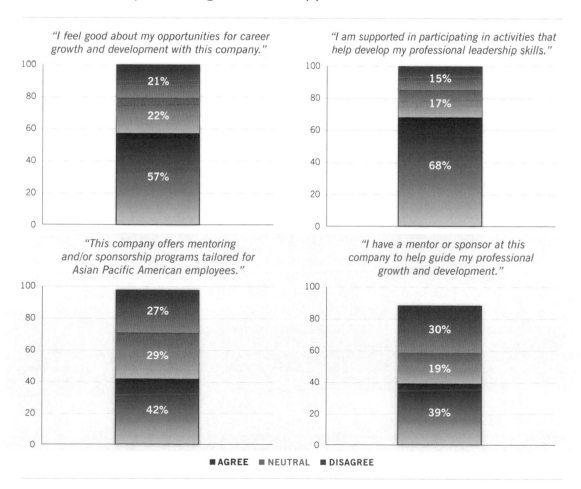

"I feel good about my opportunities for career growth and development with this company."

21%	
22%	
57%	

"I am supported in participating in activities that help develop my professional leadership skills."

15%	
17%	
68%	

"This company offers mentoring and/or sponsorship programs tailored for Asian Pacific American employees."

27%	
29%	
42%	

"I have a mentor or sponsor at this company to help guide my professional growth and development."

30%	
19%	
39%	

■ AGREE ■ NEUTRAL ■ DISAGREE

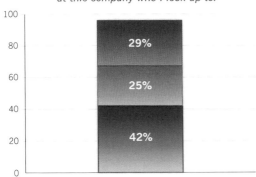

"There are Asian Pacific American role models at this company who I look up to."

29%

25%

42%

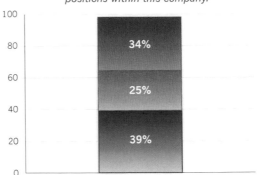

"Asian Pacific American employees have a clear presence in senior leadership positions within this company."

34%

25%

39%

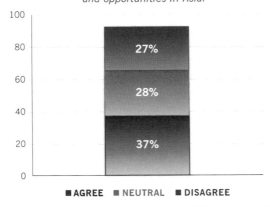

"This company encourages employees to pursue international assignments and opportunities in Asia."

27%

28%

37%

■ AGREE   ■ NEUTRAL   ■ DISAGREE

Among all survey dimensions, Professional Growth and Development received the lowest approval rating among APA employees, with mentoring and sponsorship opportunities, APA role models and leadership team representation as key areas contributing most to its low-ranking position.

Only 42% of APA employees report that their companies have APA role models.

The generally positive sentiment expressed for career growth and development opportunities (57 percent) and leadership-skills training (68 percent) is tempered by the fact that only 42 percent of APA employees report that their companies offer APA role models or mentoring/sponsorship programs designed for them. Compounding the problem, a mere 39 percent of respondents have a company mentor or sponsor, or believe APAs are visible at the company's senior levels.

Takeaways: These findings reveal that companies need to ensure that mentoring and sponsorships are prominently featured in their professional development policies and communicated to all employees, and that APA employees are informed of the benefits and opportunities.

It is also important that APA employees across levels seek out and serve as role models for fellow APAs, and that company leadership brings a renewed focus to APA representation in senior levels. Taking these steps will not only heighten APA engagement and visibility throughout the organization but will also demonstrate the company's diversity program at work.

Commitment to the APA Community Internally and Externally:
ERG and Networking Support Validated, External Efforts May Require Different Focus

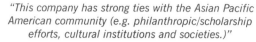
"This company has strong ties with the Asian Pacific American community (e.g. philanthropic/scholarship efforts, cultural institutions and societies.)"

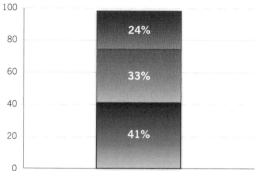

"This company supports Asian Pacific American employee resource groups."

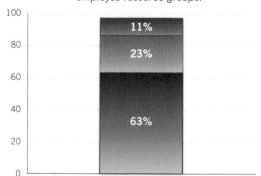

"Opportunities to network with other Asian Pacific Americans are available at this company."

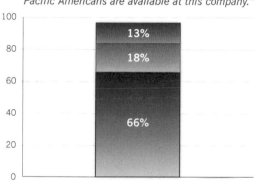

"This company's activities with the Asian Pacific American community are business-relevant and go beyond celebrations of Asian holidays and festivals."

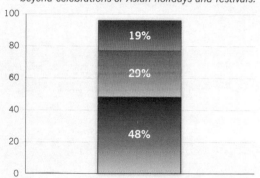

■ AGREE ■ NEUTRAL ■ DISAGREE

Within the favorable 61 percent finding for Commitment to the APA Community lies a sharp and noteworthy divide between their internal and external community efforts.

With 63 percent of respondents agreeing that their company supports APA employee resource groups, and a slightly higher 66 percent believing the same about available opportunities to network with their APA colleagues, companies are fully demonstrating their internal commitment to APA employees. However, they are achieving less impressive results beyond the confines of the organization.

> **APA employees seem to want their company's activities with the external APA community to be more business relevant.**

Only 41 percent of APA employees agree that their company's philanthropic, community and similar efforts are forging a strong relationship with the APA community. A higher, though still modest 48 percent, believe their company's APA activities are business relevant and extend beyond cultural celebrations.

Takeaways: To close the internal/external gap, and more meaningfully demonstrate their commitment to APAs, companies should bring a business-relevant element to their external outreach efforts to the APA community. Successful steps they can take range from building leadership skills and broadening expertise areas for APAs to creating programs with strategic partners.

Leadership and Company Image:
Strategic Efforts to Understand Asian Markets Need to Be Applied to Better Understand the APA Market

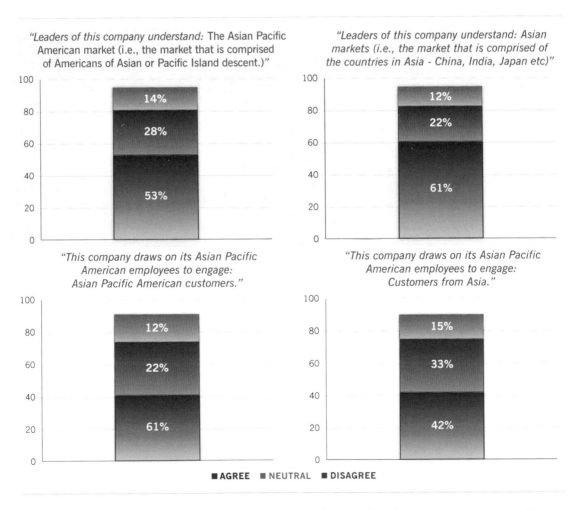

The majority of survey participants have a favorable image of their company and leadership. However, they have identified an unequal level of understanding by company leaders of the APA and Asian markets. APA employees also believe that leaders are not leveraging the unique talents, insights and competitive advantage of their APA team members to inform and benefit the company's effort to understand APA customers or customers from Asia.

Only 53 percent of respondents agree that their company leaders have an understanding of the APA market as compared to 61 percent for Asian markets. These findings point to the issue that companies may need to invest the same amount of resources to understanding the APA market as they do with Asian markets. However, these findings represent aggregate responses from APAs from all represented companies and not the individual market focus for each company. Therefore specific actions that need to be taken should be prioritized through that market focus.

Also, well under half (41 percent) of APAs agree that their company draws on APA employees when engaging APA customers, with only a slightly higher percentage (42 percent) believing so when working with customers from Asia.

> **Companies are not doing enough to draw on the expertise and knowledge of their APA employees—who represent untapped potential for companies.**

These findings represent untapped potential and competitive advantage for companies as well as significant lost opportunities, especially since few APAs responded that their company's leadership has communicated strong growth strategies in the APA market (50 percent) versus Asia (60 percent). This despite the fact that the APA market grew almost 43 percent from 2000 to 2010 according to the U.S. Census.

In addition, with only 39 percent of APAs agreeing that their company is proactive in working with APA suppliers, the survey underscores the undiscovered benefits that APAs outside the organization can bring to the company.

Takeaway: By asking senior and mid-level leaders to make a more dedicated effort identifying and using the full range of APA educational resources and talents, companies can better mobilize and apply the unique insights, skills and resources needed for growth in the U.S. and Asia.

The Job Itself:
Overall Satisfaction, But A Warning on APA Potential

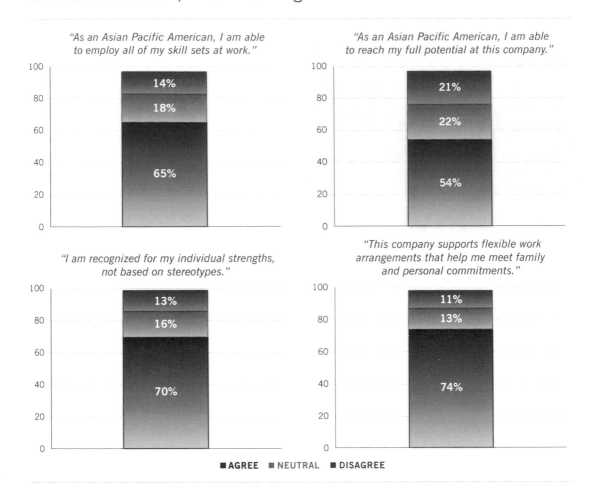

"As an Asian Pacific American, I am able to employ all of my skill sets at work."

14%
18%
65%

"As an Asian Pacific American, I am able to reach my full potential at this company."

21%
22%
54%

"I am recognized for my individual strengths, not based on stereotypes."

13%
16%
70%

"This company supports flexible work arrangements that help me meet family and personal commitments."

11%
13%
74%

■ AGREE ■ NEUTRAL ■ DISAGREE

APA employees are largely satisfied with their jobs and believe their individual strengths are recognized, free of stereotypes. 65 percent of respondents agree that as APAs they are able to apply all their skills to their job responsibilities, and 70 percent agree they are recognized for individual strengths. However, a little more than half, 54 percent, believe that as APAs, they are able to achieve their full potential at their company. These findings indicate that companies may be more successful creating an overall supportive environment in a holistic sense; but when it comes to APAs' specific job needs, there is room for improvement, especially in terms of providing growth opportunities that would allow them to reach the utmost limits of their abilities. The desire for more specific growth and job opportunities may be more clearly reflected in the lower scores within the Professional Growth and Development dimension.

The Job Itself dimension is directly linked to Professional Growth and Development dimension.

Takeaway: Employers have made largely successful efforts to create an aspirational work environment. However, more focus needs to be placed on specific resources such as training, guidance and advancement opportunities, that will help employees achieve those aspirations. In doing so, they can increase overall APA engagement and satisfaction levels as well.

Satisfaction, Commitment and Belonging:
Loyalty is Not Translating into A Sense of Belonging for APA Employees

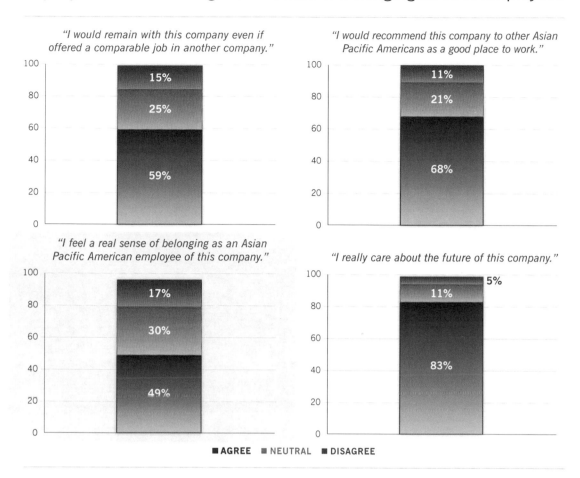

"I would remain with this company even if offered a comparable job in another company."

15%
25%
59%

"I would recommend this company to other Asian Pacific Americans as a good place to work."

11%
21%
68%

"I feel a real sense of belonging as an Asian Pacific American employee of this company."

17%
30%
49%

"I really care about the future of this company."

5%
11%
83%

■ **AGREE** ■ NEUTRAL ■ DISAGREE

As in previous years, APA employees are generally satisfied with their employers and demonstrate their satisfaction in ways ranging from company loyalty to recommending the organization to other APAs as a good place to work. While these findings support APAs' commitment to their job and organization, there remains one area that warrants greater consideration.

83 percent of survey participants care about their company's future, which demonstrates a high degree of current engagement and respect for the organization. However, despite having such a strong loyalty to their company, less than half (49 percent) feel a sense of belonging as an APA employee.

> **Despite great loyalty, APA employees do not feel a sense of belonging at their companies.**

This feeling of not belonging can be attributed to many concrete factors discussed in previous dimensions, such as: the lack of APA role models and mentors, low APA representation in the company's leadership ranks, and feelings that companies do not value their skills and experience as Asian Pacific Americans in the context of conducting business. This is especially important, as this dimension serves largely as a proxy for overall APA employee satisfaction and can thus be a gauge for progress. Takeaway: It is only by addressing elements within the other dimensions, that companies can improve Satisfaction, Commitment and Belonging.

Analysis of Trends

American Identity a Factor in APA Engagement

Survey results were analyzed from the perspective of a number of different key demographics—Time in the U.S., Age of Arrival in the U.S., Executive Leadership Track and Job Level, Gender, Age, and Years with Current Employer. This analysis underscores the influence that personal experiences and characteristics have on the most important workplace issues for APAs. The findings clearly show that in many cases, demographic issues have a significant influence on APA employees' job satisfaction and engagement levels.

Perceived differences by country of origin seem in large part, to be explained by differences within these demographic variables. For example, though APAs of Chinese origin seem to rate their companies less favorably, as in 2011, the vast majority of these employees were either born in the U.S. or have been here for over 20 years—groups with lower favorability scores overall.

Time in the U.S. (Years)

One of the survey's most significant findings continues to be that the longer APAs are in the U.S., the greater the decline in positive responses across every workplace dimension. The most measurable declines occur in Professional Growth and Development (15 percent) and Leadership and Company Image (14 percent).

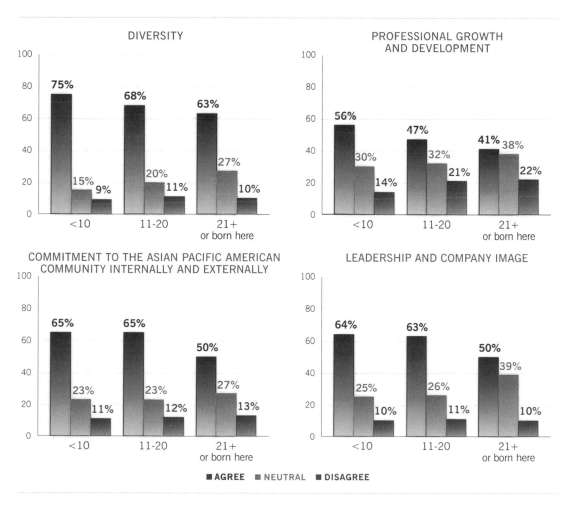

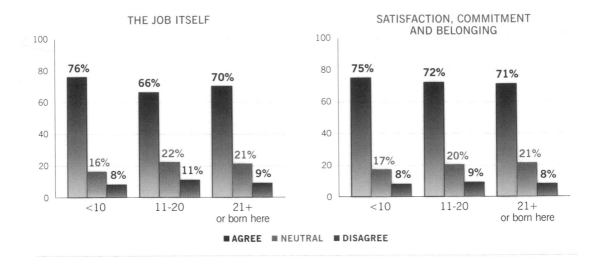

THE JOB ITSELF

SATISFACTION, COMMITMENT AND BELONGING

■ AGREE   ■ NEUTRAL   ■ DISAGREE

> **The longer APAs are in the U.S. the greater the decline in positive responses across every workplace dimension—especially within Professional Growth and Development.**

To determine whether there is a connection between the decline and longevity in the U.S., or whether other factors are involved, the survey examined more deeply the group of employees who were not born in the U.S. Comparing APA responses based on the age they arrived in the U.S.—broadly defined as *"Childhood"* (younger than 10 years old), *"Teen"* (10 to 20 years old) and "Adult" (21 years old and up)—a similar decline in favorability became apparent for those who arrived as children rather than as teens and adults.

The lone exception is The Job Itself, where the 73 percent satisfaction level in the Childhood category exceeds all others—Teen (69 percent) and Adult (67 percent).

Age of Arrival in U.S.

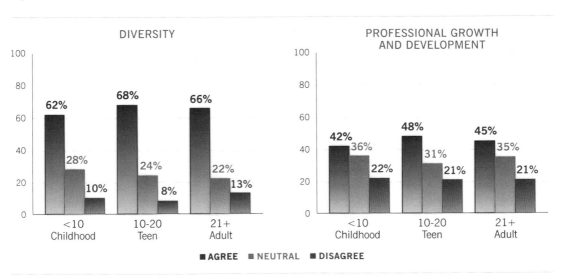

DIVERSITY

PROFESSIONAL GROWTH AND DEVELOPMENT

■ AGREE   ■ NEUTRAL   ■ DISAGREE

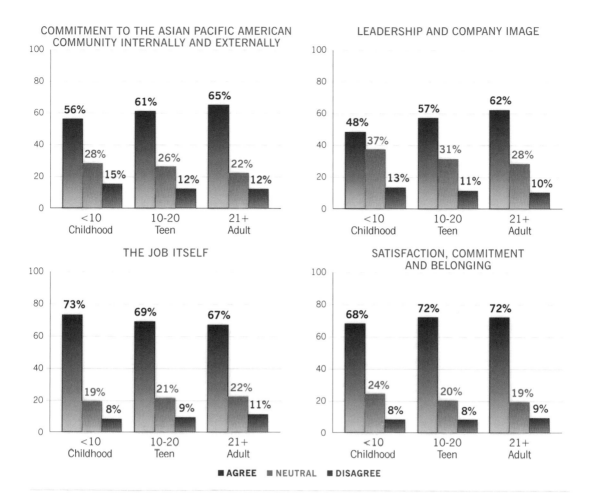

COMMITMENT TO THE ASIAN PACIFIC AMERICAN COMMUNITY INTERNALLY AND EXTERNALLY

LEADERSHIP AND COMPANY IMAGE

THE JOB ITSELF

SATISFACTION, COMMITMENT AND BELONGING

■ AGREE ■ NEUTRAL ■ DISAGREE

This data indicates that the decline in favorability is not a simple factor of longevity in this country and is, perhaps, due to having an American identity.

Decline in favorability could be due to increasing American identity.

American identity is defined, for purposes of this report, as having an inherent understanding of the unspoken rules and idiosyncrasies of American culture, i.e., being culturally *"native."* This definition extends beyond feelings of patriotism or specific U.S. citizenship status, and it can be assumed that those native born APAs or those who arrived as children have a greater American identity.

APAs with less time in the U.S., or who moved to the U.S. later in life, have higher satisfaction due to different priorities and less awareness or focus on the inequities they encounter.

Takeaway: APAs with a strong American identity share the same job and career expectations as their non-APA counterparts. This identity makes them more aware of the workplace inequities they face. The result is overall erosion in the optimism and enthusiasm they had at the start of their career.

An Internal Satisfaction Divide

To distinguish between APA employees at various levels of their organization, the survey asked specific questions about employee titles and positions within their companies. Those who answered "Yes" to either of the following questions, differed significantly from those who answered "No":

- ▶ People with my title or similar titles can become part of the senior leadership of my company.
- ▶ My title or similar titles are executive/senior leadership titles.

"People with my title or similar titles can become part of the senior leadership of my company."

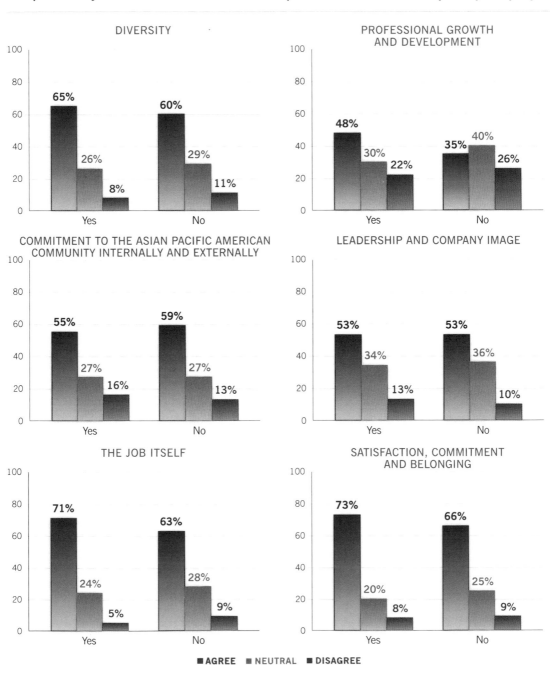

DIVERSITY

PROFESSIONAL GROWTH AND DEVELOPMENT

COMMITMENT TO THE ASIAN PACIFIC AMERICAN COMMUNITY INTERNALLY AND EXTERNALLY

LEADERSHIP AND COMPANY IMAGE

THE JOB ITSELF

SATISFACTION, COMMITMENT AND BELONGING

■ AGREE ■ NEUTRAL ■ DISAGREE

"My title or similar titles are executive/senior leadership titles"

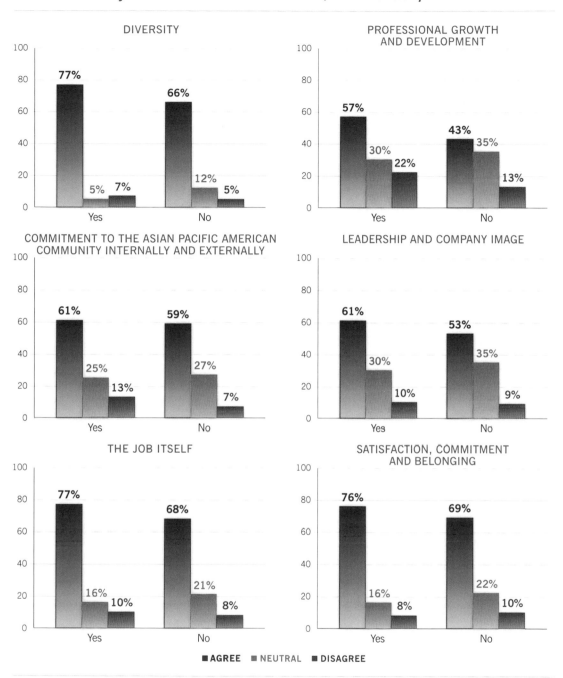

DIVERSITY
- Yes: 77%, 5%, 7%
- No: 66%, 12%, 5%

PROFESSIONAL GROWTH AND DEVELOPMENT
- Yes: 57%, 30%, 22%
- No: 43%, 35%, 13%

COMMITMENT TO THE ASIAN PACIFIC AMERICAN COMMUNITY INTERNALLY AND EXTERNALLY
- Yes: 61%, 25%, 13%
- No: 59%, 27%, 7%

LEADERSHIP AND COMPANY IMAGE
- Yes: 61%, 30%, 10%
- No: 53%, 35%, 9%

THE JOB ITSELF
- Yes: 77%, 16%, 10%
- No: 68%, 21%, 8%

SATISFACTION, COMMITMENT AND BELONGING
- Yes: 76%, 16%, 8%
- No: 69%, 22%, 10%

■AGREE ■NEUTRAL ■DISAGREE

The greatest disparity (48 percent vs. 35 Percent) occurs in two dimensions—professional growth and development, and commitment to the APA community internally and externally.

Survey results reveal that across almost every survey dimension, those who answered "Yes" hold their jobs and workplaces in higher esteem. The dimension where the divide separating the two types of respondents is most obvious can be found in Professional Growth and Development (14 percent spread) and in Diversity (11 percent spread).

Satisfaction divide is not necessarily APA-specific.

This is a situation where observed differences in APA employee responses do not necessarily indicate an APA-specific problem. All companies send both overt and covert signals that *"revenue producers"* or *"client-facing"* employees are valued, for example in terms of salary, benefits, title and other workplace features. It is therefore not surprising that these employees would feel more positive about their companies. The same hold true for employees who see themselves as potential future leaders of the company. Takeaway: Since the gap in satisfaction is not APA-specific, a company's efforts to improve this situation for all employees would positively affect APA employees as well.

Surprising Similarity in Favorability by Gender Merits Further Study

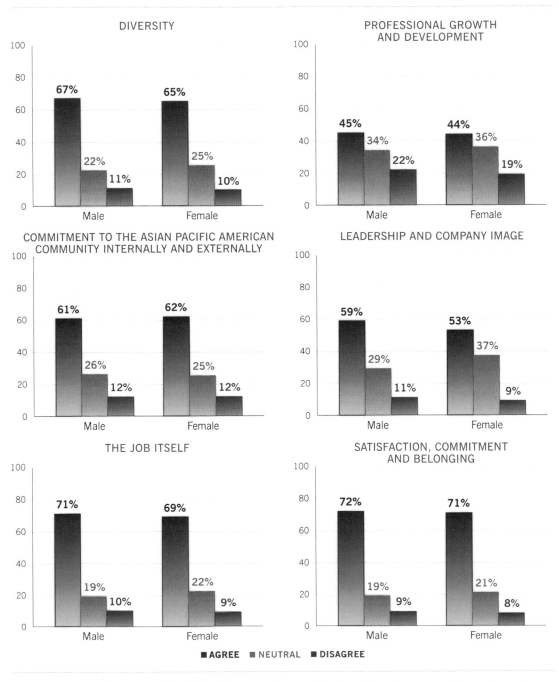

The dramatic differences of opinion that are observed in the other demographic analyses do not appear to apply to gender, this year.

Across the dimensions, male and female APAs predominantly share the same opinions on key career and company issues. This consistency in responses reflects a shared degree of satisfaction between genders.

The number of programs directed toward the specific needs of minority women in the workplace, for example in the Best Practices section of this report, indicate that companies are aware of a gender divide that does not seem to show up in the survey results this year. In fact, the 2011 APA Survey indicated that APA men viewed their companies more favorably consistently across all dimensions. The differences were small, but were in most cases statistically significant.

Decreasing Satisfaction and Engagement with Age

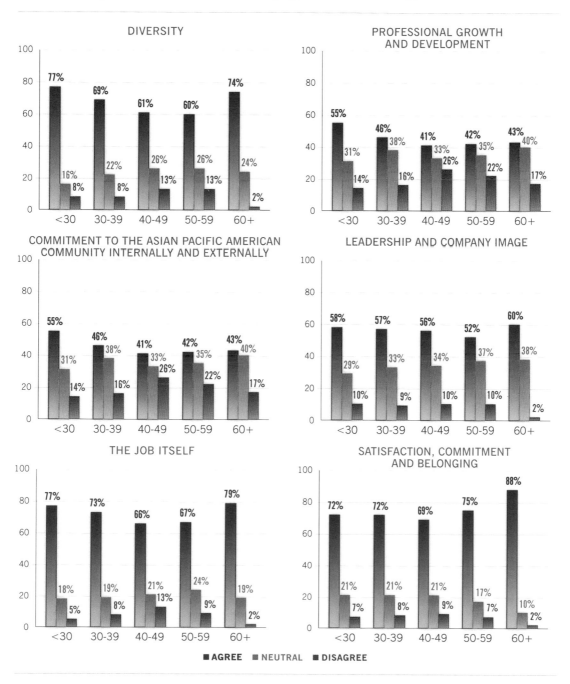

Younger APA employees who are new to the job market are generally more optimistic about key workplace features than their more experienced colleagues. This is a sentiment likely shared by non-APA employees.

The large percentage of *"Agree"* responses in this first category (less than 30 years old), may be due to the optimism of all new entrants to the workforce, regardless of race. At this stage, plans and expectations run high for raises, promotions, network-building and challenging assignments. Also, during these early career phases, initial and mid-level goals become achieved more easily and quickly. For APA employees this is when the perception of them being good "implementers" eases the promotion path.

From age 30 to 59, job satisfaction levels gradually taper off until age 60 and over, when favorability scores begin to climb, especially in The Job Itself (12 percent), Satisfaction, Commitment and Belonging (13 percent) and Diversity (14 percent).

> **APA employees show declining engagement at the critical juncture between middle management and senior management, possibly due to inequities in treatment.**

This reflects the experience of APAs as they move up the career ladder. From 30 to 59 years old, most professionals make the transition from middle to senior management. It is also the time when the decline in APA employee job satisfaction begins to take hold. Relationships and other intangible factors now become paramount for advancement. These are the same factors that have historically been difficult for APAs and other groups to access. Takeaway: When APA employees encounter obstacles to advancement because of the lack of these career-building intangibles, they experience lowered optimism, satisfaction and engagement.

Ironically, satisfaction levels for APAs age 60 and over exceed those for the less than 30 age group in three dimensions—Leadership and Company Image, The Job Itself, and especially Overall Satisfaction, which shows an impressive 16 percent climb.

As retirement begins to come into view, priorities start to shift from raises and new responsibilities to pending retirement and new horizons, which possibly change their focus to quality of life and possibly a less corporate and a more entrepreneurial lifestyle. This shifting of priorities occurs for all employees.

The Age analysis also seems to explain observed differences according to Years With Current Employer. In our sample, those who have been with their companies the least amount of time are also generally younger.

Engagement Drivers

Engagement Drivers Remain the Same

The top ten engagement drivers[1] in 2012 were the same as in 2011, though their relative ranking has changed slightly. *"Career growth and development"* is number one again this year, and the ability to *"reach my full potential"* is ranked second again. The consistency in the engagement drivers indicates the need for sustained long-term programming to address them and thus improve engagement.

The Top 10 Drivers for APA Employee Engagement
RANKED BY ORDER OF IMPORTANCE

1	I feel good about my opportunities for career growth and development with this company.
2	As an Asian Pacific American, I am able to reach my full potential at this company.
3	I am recognized for individual strengths, not based on stereotypes.
4	As an Asian Pacific American, I am able to employ all of my skill sets at work.
5	I am supported in participating in activities that help develop my professional leadership skills.
6	This company's efforts to develop Asian Pacific Americans are fully supported by supervisors and employees.
7	My company's mission statement articulates a commitment to creating and maintaining a diverse workforce inclusive of all groups.
8	Promotions are awarded to the most deserving employees, regardless of gender, ethnicity, etc.
9	The company supports flexible work arrangements that help me meet family and personal commitments.
10	I work in an environment that is free from disrespectful and offensive behavior toward Asian Pacific Americans.

1. Engagement drivers were determined using logistic regression modeling.

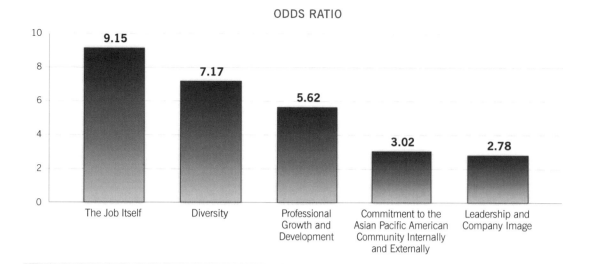

Measuring the Positive Effects of Diversity

Analysis of 2012 APA survey data explored the individual relationships between the Satisfaction, Commitment and Belonging dimension, as a proxy for the core elements of employee satisfaction, and all others. Each of the other dimensions was significantly correlated to satisfaction, indicating that all were linked. Focusing on any one of these dimensions could help to increase satisfaction from a statistical sense. The salient question for companies becomes how to increase employee satisfaction in PRACTICAL terms.

A Mandate for Individualized Approaches

The additional analysis uncovered that increasing satisfaction within the Job Itself dimension increases the odds of overall satisfaction 9 times. However, achieving the desired increase can be elusive for the vast majority of companies, largely because of the difficulty in creating programs that respond directly to the components of this dimension. For example, what are the elements of a program that makes employees feel that they can reach their "full potential"?

> **Satisfaction within the job itself dimension increases the odds of overall satisfaction 9 times, but it is difficult to influence this dimension directly.**

This demonstrates the need to focus on components of the other dimensions. Professional Growth and Development, Commitment to the APA Community Internally and Externally, and Leadership and Company Image, all influence The Job Itself. Ameliorating these can help achieve high satisfaction overall among APA employees.

Established Foundation Reinforces the Need for More Personalized Approaches

The Diversity dimension presents different challenges. In this instance companies have already made great strides, from human resource policies to cultural sensitivity training. While this does not mean that companies have solved the issue of diversity, it does suggest that the basic foundations for doing so are in place for companies at the Fortune 500 level. Therefore, to increase satisfaction amongst APA employees (and probably other employees as well), companies must again turn to the other dimensions to make an impact.

Pathway to Increasing APA Employee Satisfaction

Having established that companies need to look to dimensions other than The Job Itself and
Diversity to increase APA employee satisfaction, what do the other dimensions suggest in
terms of strategic action steps?

Professional Growth and Development

Strategic Action Steps:

> ► Offer career growth and development opportunities to APA employees.
>
> ► Support APAs' participation in leadership skills-building activities.
>
> ► Create a clear presence of APA employees in senior leadership positions.

Commitment to APA Community Internally and Externally

Strategic Action Steps:

> ► Establish and maintain strong ties with the APA community.
>
> ► Support APA Employee Resource Groups.
>
> ► Offer business-relevant activities with the APA community, which extend beyond holiday
> and festival celebrations.

Leadership and Company Image

Strategic Action Steps:

> ► Build a positive image in the APA community.
>
> ► Ensure that company leaders understand the APA market.
>
> ► Ensure that company leaders understand Asian markets.

The Best Practices section of this report showcases exactly how some of the participating
companies have brought these action steps to life.

Best in Class

Finalist companies were selected by using a weighted formula. 80 percent of the final score came from the employee survey responses. 20 percent of the final score was determined by a judging panel, comprised of four experts in diversity leadership. Each panel member reviewed submissions from each finalist.

Finalist Companies:
Cardinal Health, Inc., Cisco, Colgate-Palmolive Company, Corning Incorporated, Eli Lilly and Company, Freddie Mac, GE, Goldman, Sachs & Co., IBM, KPMG LLP, Merck, New York Life Insurance Company, Pfizer, PG&E Corporation and Sodexo.

Company identification information was concealed from the panel members in order to ensure objectivity in ratings. The gap between corporate policies/programs (as evidenced by the application form that was completed by the company's diversity leadership) and actual APA employee experiences (as measured by the scores given by employees of the company who took the survey) was a key factor in the ratings.

Best in Class companies were selected from among the finalists using a weighted formula and represent the aggregate scores of the Award Winners and the Distinguished Practice honorees.

Best in Class Companies:
Continuing Investment in Growth and Development

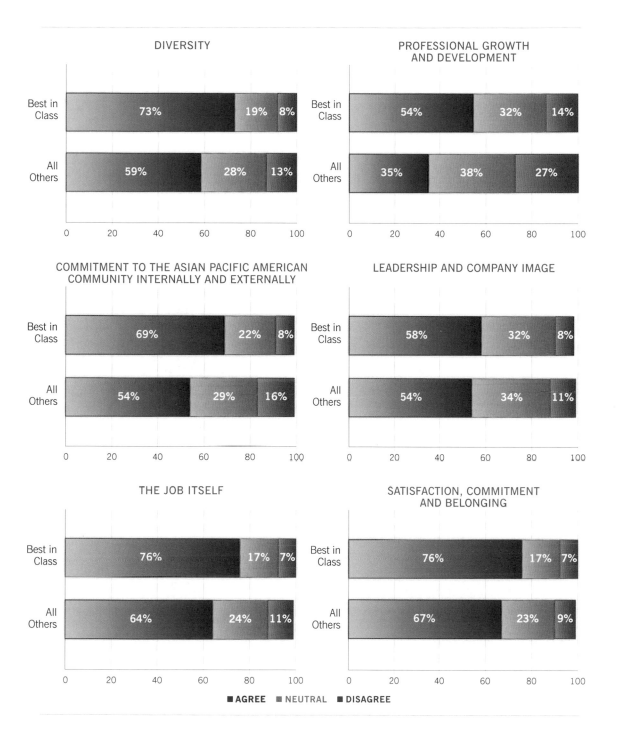

DIVERSITY

Best in Class	73%	19% 8%
All Others	59%	28% 13%

PROFESSIONAL GROWTH AND DEVELOPMENT

Best in Class	54%	32% 14%
All Others	35%	38% 27%

COMMITMENT TO THE ASIAN PACIFIC AMERICAN COMMUNITY INTERNALLY AND EXTERNALLY

Best in Class	69%	22% 8%
All Others	54%	29% 16%

LEADERSHIP AND COMPANY IMAGE

Best in Class	58%	32% 8%
All Others	54%	34% 11%

THE JOB ITSELF

Best in Class	76%	17% 7%
All Others	64%	24% 11%

SATISFACTION, COMMITMENT AND BELONGING

Best in Class	76%	17% 7%
All Others	67%	23% 9%

■ AGREE ■ NEUTRAL ■ DISAGREE

The 2012 Best in Class companies were again viewed significantly better by their employees on every dimension. The biggest differences seen were in the dimensions of Diversity (14 percentage points higher for Best in Class companies), Commitment to the Community (15 percentage points) and Professional Growth and Development (19 percentage points).

The gap between the Best in Class and the other companies has in general, persisted at the same levels in 2012. Notably however, the two groups are essentially at parity on the dimension of Leadership and Company Image, as opposed to a 15 percentage point advantage for Best in Class in 2011. The gap also decreased slightly for Commitment to the

APA community, suggesting that companies' efforts along these two dimensions are bearing fruit. It will be interesting to note whether this improvement continues.

Most importantly, along the dimension of Professional Growth and Development, a majority of Best in Class company employees (54 percent)still have a positive perception of this dimension. In contrast, in "All Other" companies this drops to just 35 percent. This may indicate that the programs in this dimension remain a priority for Best in Class companies and they may be maintaining these programs, despite budgetary pressures from the recent recession.

A deeper look at specific components within each dimension provides a clearer picture of why Best in Class companies continue to lead. The most interesting factors are those where Best in Class companies are near 50 percent or above, though additional elements are also relevant.

	% AGREE	
QUESTION	BEST IN CLASS	OTHERS
Professional Growth and Development		
This company offers mentoring and/or sponsorship programs tailored for Asian Pacific American employees.	50%	34%
I have a mentor or sponsor at this company to help guide my professional growth and development.	46	33
There are Asian Pacific American role models at this company who I look up to.	49	35
Asian Pacific American employees have a clear presence in senior leadership positions within this company.	48	30
Leadership and Company Image		
This company's activities with the Asian Pacific American community are business-relevant and go beyond celebrations of Asian holidays and festivals.	55	42
This company draws on its Asian Pacific American employees to engage: Asian Pacific American customers.	48	34
This company draws on its Asian Pacific American employees to engage: Customers from Asia.	46	38
This company has a positive image in the Asian Pacific American community.	60	49
Satisfaction, Commitment and Belonging		
As an Asian Pacific American, I am able to reach my full potential at this company.	62	46
I feel a real sense of belonging as an Asian Pacific American employee of this company.	56	42

Broadly, Best in Class companies make their APA employees feel more valued. The direct questions related to this—*"having a sense of belonging"* or being *"able to reach their full potential"*—exhibit this clearly, with Best in Class scores 16 and 14 points higher than other companies, respectively. More powerful are the scores where actions on the part of the company are more tangible, for example APAs in senior leadership positions and the existence of APA role models. In addition, the higher scores that Best in Class APA employees give to *"business relevance of activities with the Asian Pacific American community"* reinforce the importance of going beyond simple awareness events, into more strategic partnerships that benefit the employees in terms of professional development.

> **Best in Class companies make their APA employees feel more valued.**

The issue of mentoring and sponsorship merits special discussion, given the recognized connection between these relationships and employee engagement. While 50 percent of Best in Class company employees agree that their companies have a mentoring or sponsorship program, this figure is only 34 percent at other companies. And, 46 percent of employees of the Best in Class companies have a mentor or sponsor. Takeaway: One thing companies can do is increase the availability and uptake of their mentoring/sponsorship programs, as well as maintain growth and development plans more generally.

Engagement Drivers—One Important Differentiator
Unsurprisingly, engagement drivers are similar for both Best in Class and other companies, though the specific order differs somewhat. However, as indicated in the dimensions discussion, Best in Class companies seem to have better mastered engaging and valuing the skills and talents of APA employees. Thus these companies have *"In our work group, we capitalize on the perspectives and talents of Asian Pacific American employees in accomplishing objectives,"* as an engagement driver.

Other companies have *"an environment free from disrespectful behavior"* and *"image in the APA community"* as drivers, indicating that these macro-level issues are still a concern. This is in comparison with Best in Class companies whose employees are focused on job-specific concerns and policies.

Best in Class Engagement Drivers	All Other Companies Engagement Drivers
I am recognized for individual strengths, not based on stereotypes.	As an Asian Pacific American, I am able to employ all of my skill sets at work.
I feel good about my opportunities for career growth and development with this company.	I feel good about my opportunities for career growth and development with this company.
As an Asian Pacific American, I am able to reach my full potential at this company.	As an Asian Pacific American, I am able to reach my full potential at this company.
As an Asian Pacific American, I am able to employ all of my skill sets at work.	I am recognized for individual strengths, not based on stereotypes.
This company's efforts to develop Asian Pacific Americans are fully supported by supervisors and employees.	I am supported in participating in activities that help develop my professional leadership skills.
I am supported in participating in activities that help develop my professional leadership skills.	This company's efforts to develop Asian Pacific Americans are fully supported by supervisors and employees.
My company's mission statement articulates a commitment to creating and maintaining a diverse workforce inclusive of all groups.	My company's mission statement articulates a commitment to creating and maintaining a diverse workforce inclusive of all groups.
In our work group, we capitalize on the perspectives and talents of Asian Pacific American employees in accomplishing objectives.	I work in an environment that is free from disrespectful and offensive behavior toward Asian Pacific Americans.
Promotions are awarded to the most deserving employees, regardless of gender, ethnicity, etc.	Promotions are awarded to the most deserving employees, regardless of gender, ethnicity, etc.
The company supports flexible work arrangements that help me meet family and personal commitments.	The company has a positive image in the Asian Pacific American community.

Best Practices

Best Practices were chosen by the Awards Panel from all company submissions of the APA Survey. Professionals within each company's Diversity & Inclusion department were asked to answer open-ended questions about their programming that benefitted their APA employees. This enabled companies who were not able to participate in the employee portion of the survey were included. Each panel member selected his or her top five programs within each of the dimensions examined:

- ► Mentoring and Sponsorship
- ► Diversity
- ► Recruitment and Selection
- ► Retention Efforts
- ► Employee Growth and Advancement
- ► Work-Life Effectiveness
- ► Support for the Community.

Submissions were judged according to innovation and impact. Importantly, scores from the employee portion of the survey were not considered. The rankings were indexed and re-ranked. The panel as a whole used this re-ranking and additional discussion, to come to agreement on the Best Practices within each dimension.

Mentoring & Sponsorship:

Mentoring and sponsorship are widely recognized as crucial programs for not only APA advancement but for the advancement of all employees. The Best Practice companies integrate mentoring into overall talent management, coaching or professional development programs. Whether informal or formal, each of the companies takes its overall commitment to this dimension and translates it into expansive programs that span the company, while ensuring that the relationships developed meet the individual needs of the mentees and mentors alike.

 **KPMG LLP**'s mentoring initiatives are designed to involve all employees and partners throughout the firm. Additional efforts targeted toward diverse individuals, including Asian Pacific Americans, supplement firm-wide programs. The company offers a formal mentoring program for all employees and partners. Approximately 11,000 professionals are involved, with more than 8,000 mentoring relationships. Tools for creating and sustaining a successful mentoring relationship are housed on KPMG's Mentoring Web site, which provides mentors and mentees with guidance related to successful roles in a mentoring relationship. A National Mentor Database enables those professionals wanting to serve as a mentor to register their interest and availability.

Chapters of KPMG's Asian-Pacific Islander Network (APIN) offer numerous ways for its Asian Pacific American employees to learn more about, and get involved in, mentoring. Countless mentoring relationships-both formal and informal-have formed as a result of professionals coming together in local APIN chapters. In addition, APIN chapters have developed many special mentoring events and programs. For example, in Philadelphia, a forum was designed to match younger professionals within the APIN with more experienced colleagues who can serve as mentors.

Leaders Engaging Leaders is a career-advising program that establishes one-to-one mentoring relationships between members of KPMG's Board of Directors and Management Committee, and high-performing diverse partners, including Asian Pacific Americans. Participants receive guidance, championing and career support from a highly senior professional in order to prepare them for a client or operational leadership role. The program has recently expanded to increase the number of participants.

An important factor within KPMG's mentoring programs is the recognition of the mentors themselves. Each year the company asks mentees to nominate their mentor(s) for the KPMG National Mentoring Award. The firm formally recognizes about 20 mentors each year with this honor.

Lastly, the company's Key Accounts Rotation Program is an initiative designed to enrich the careers of ethnically diverse associates, including Asian Pacific Americans, by ensuring that they have opportunities to participate in "priority" client engagements that are important to career advancement. The program helps ensure that young professionals receive high-profile client exposure and the broad range of experiences necessary to build critical skills, as well as opportunities to develop relationships with influential KPMG partners. In fiscal year 2011, nearly all of KPMG's diverse associates served on at least one priority account engagement.

 **Pfizer** established mentoring as a core component of its integrated talent management strategy and as a key ingredient of developing talent in 2010. Employees can access information about mentoring including the responsibilities of a good mentor, the role of a mentee, best practices for forming mentoring relationships, insights and tips on cross-cultural mentoring, as well as the differences between a mentor and a sponsor. MentorMatch, their online mentoring program and resource site, guides users so they can find or be a mentor and develop the strongest mentoring relationships. MentorMatch is one of the many resources and tools available globally to colleagues within a comprehensive online career development resource center.

Pfizer's Global Asian Alliance (GAA) ensures that the availability of various mentoring, career-planning and talent-development tools is communicated broadly within the Asian Pacific American (APA) community. For example GAA's New York Chapter, APAG, has also established a group mentoring process for some of the more senior members in their Asian Pacific American Group led by executive sponsor Sally Susman, who is EVP of Policy, External Affairs and Communications, a member of the Executive Leadership team and direct report of the CEO. Responding to research that APAG performed on the developmental needs of its members, "Sally's Circles" as they are known, focused on self-advocacy. Based on positive feedback from program participants, the program is being broadened for the coming year and is a model for other diverse groups as well.

Ed Gadsden, Chief Diversity Officer, Pfizer noted that it was *"very impactful for a senior executive in the company to actually spend the time to lead and support this initiative. Her presence and energy really helped shaped how participants felt about the program."*

Finally, many of Pfizer's APA High Potentials (HiPos) participate in a broader Senior Leader mentoring effort, designed to create mentoring relationships that may evolve into sponsorship relationships. HiPos are matched with senior leader mentors based on their individual development needs as identified in their Individual Development Plan (IDP's).

Goldman Sachs

Goldman, Sachs & Co. takes an expansive view of professional development and recognizes that facilitating mentorship relationships is a key development component. The infrastructure to support mentoring programs includes an in-house mentoring training curriculum, a standard evaluation tool, a best practices guide to creating a mentoring program and a website. Also, a diversity mentoring toolkit was created to address specific mentoring issues.

Mentoring initiatives are well-integrated into the firm's talent management processes. Each year the firm conducts a senior talent review during which divisional and regional leaders discuss key talent with an executive office talent committee. Divisional and regional leadership assess their employees' potential and performance, including crucial mentor and/or sponsor action steps for each division.

Mentorship relationships are tracked through the career development reviews conducted annually and the firm's comprehensive 360-degree performance review. Individuals without mentors are encouraged to find one or are assigned mentors through a formal process when possible. In 2011, 22 percent of all employees who received mentoring in the U.S. were Asian, and 86 percent of Asian employees in the U.S. had career conversations with their managers.

APA Network events encourage junior professionals to leverage network activities in order to seek out more seasoned professionals as mentors. For example, a formal reverse mentoring program launched by the Operations Division Asian Professionals Network is being expanded in 2012. The Doors Wide Open program creates an opportunity for APA employees to connect with the firm's activities and senior leaders in Asia. Women in Technology (WIT 2.0), helps women at all levels of the technology organization share concerns, leverage their strengths and prepare for new opportunities. In addition, divisional network heads/co-heads are typically selected from the pool of high-potential, high-performing senior vice presidents and given unique access to their divisional leaders and key decision makers through their role as network co-heads.

> Edith Hunt, Chief Diversity Officer, Goldman Sachs: *"For a company like Goldman Sachs, success is dependent upon our people. For career advancement and talent development, we've long recognized that training is necessary but not sufficient. Mentoring is crucial in developing the interpersonal skills necessary for leadership."*

Lastly, the Multicultural Women's Initiative (MWI) focuses on enhancing the workplace experience for Asian, African-American, Hispanic and Native American women at Goldman Sachs and in the financial services industry. Initially begun as an internal program, MWI now has more than 80 involved companies. Programs include a nomination-based talent management program, a quarterly forum for associates and vice presidents to engage with senior leaders, and an external-facing program focused on commercial and professional development.

CORNING

At **Corning Incorporated**, mentoring is viewed as a complementary development tool with coaching. Together they provide a beneficial process of pairing an individual with specific learning goals. An important factor in Corning's mentoring and coaching success is the number of APA employees in leadership positions of their affinity groups. Close to 20 percent of affinity group leadership identifies as APA. This means that the pool of potential mentors, role models and sponsors is relatively large. Leadership participation rates for APA employees are similar to or greater than those of other diverse groups.

As an affinity group leader, APA employees can participate in a number of mentoring and coaching programs such as the Affinity Group Leaders Forum. It also allows them to participate in the speed networking program, which provides critical introductions and connections to senior leaders outside their home divisions.

Measurement and tracking of mentoring is also important. Affinity group leadership and participation is integrated into Corning's Manage by Objective system. Employees can allocate up to 10 percent of their annual objectives for a leadership role in an Affinity Group and 5 percent for membership involvement in an Affinity group. By doing this employees are required to measure and track what they hope to gain from a developmental perspective.

> Debra Turner Bailey, Global Diversity Officer, Corning: *"A lot of the issues that arise in terms of employee engagement, such as relationship development often show up in diverse populations earlier or more profoundly. So when you make progress on those issues, it really enhances your overall culture."*

Innovation is equally important. For example, Corning's Speed Networking was originally designed as a novel way to introduce employees to senior leaders outside their areas of expertise. However for APA employees, many of whom are in the company's technical job families it also provided an opportunity to develop and practice their personal "elevator speech." The APA affinity group had identified personal marketing as a main growth area. What sets this program apart is the recognition by Corning of the add-on synergies to the larger employee population.

IBM The **IBM** Global Mentoring Program is based on a core set of business principles and accessible to all employees—it reflects the Diversity concept of, "Everyone is included and no one is excluded." Three categories of mentoring have been defined.

- ► Expert mentoring targets a specific skill or expertise to be transferred—technical, sales, business acumen, etc.
- ► Socialization mentoring addresses the needs of new hires to help them make a quick and smooth transition into the business.
- ► Career mentoring offers long-term career guidance.

The mentoring program is administered in a formal and structured manner, in which a specific business need is being addressed with a set of specific measurable objectives. Conversely, informal mentoring is primarily employee-driven—to help employees self-select mentors, they are provided with tools, education and resources to enable them to make the right decisions.

The Asian Pacific American Network in IBM is very active in helping its members in personal and professional development. For example, some Asian Diversity Network Groups host speed mentoring events with executives to learn more about their career journey, advise/counsel, share experiences and ask questions on career development. Cross-border mentoring with IBM colleagues in China focuses on building technical skills in new areas of business in their native language, Mandarin. Finally, in collaboration with colleges and high schools, IBM brings students on-site to shadow high potential employees and executives to gain experience in the corporate world. They are able to gain unique insights and spend a day in life of an engineer.

Business and Technical Leadership (BTL) is IBM's integrated pipeline management and succession planning process. The BTL process ensures that IBM has the right business and technical leadership talent in the appropriate key positions at the right time. It also ensures a healthy pipeline for key positions, ranging from those ready to fill key leadership positions to those expected to fill key leadership positions. This process involves a regular assessment of long-term leadership potential, focused development planning, and identification of candidates for future leadership pipelines. The goal of the Business and Technical Leadership process is to help IBM have the leadership talent to fill key positions, now and in the future, resulting in a world-class leadership team.

 At **PG&E Corporation**, much of the mentoring program is part and parcel of activities from InspirAsian (formerly Asian Employee Association), the company's 26-year old APA employee resource group. InspirAsian developed a grass roots leadership program that includes hands on learning, benchmarking, classes and mentoring matching initiatives. The participants are matched with director level and above leaders in the company to help them further develop both personally and professionally.

In 2011, the leadership program enrollees participated in a benchmarking project sponsored by the vice president of Investor Relations, They had the opportunity to present their findings to the SVP and CFO of PG&E Corporation and officer sponsor of InspirAsian. This provided great exposure for the program, as well as for the individuals who went above and beyond in developing their leadership and presentation skills.

> Michael Coyle, Principal Program Manager, Diversity & Inclusion, PG&E:
> *"A real hallmark of our programs is the face-time employees get in front of senior leaders. As in all large, complex organizations, junior and middle level employees may not even see senior executives within the normal course of their jobs. These programs help them to raise their profile."*

Separately, each of InspirAsian's Board members are also paired with one of the executive officer sponsors/advisory board members for coaching and mentoring for the two years that they are part of the leadership team.

The ERG's senior executive sponsors are strong supporters of the ERG's programs and active participants, and their long-term focus and commitment is a cornerstone of the ERG's success. For example Fong Wan, SVP of Energy Procurement has been involved with the ERG for many years and has not only made a strong effort to mention the importance of ERG involvement in his remarks and videos but he also demonstrates his beliefs through actions by participating in the group's activities.

InspirAsian ERG is also an active sponsor and partner to Ascend Pan-Asian Leaders and CAAEN (Corporate Asian American Employee Network), participating in events, seminars and conventions of these organizations, that help APA employees to develop mentoring relationships outside the firm.

Diversity

Among Fortune 500 level companies, such as those participating in this year's APA Survey, diversity efforts go far beyond non-discrimination policies. Employee resource groups, also known as employees networks, affinity groups or affinity networks, play a critical role. The programs in this section demonstrate how alignment of diversity activities with a company's business objectives results in programs that are relevant for the employees involved and also help to move the company forward in terms of its people and its bottom-line.

 GE strives to maintain a culture where every employee can grow and succeed. There are five company-sponsored affinity networks—African American Forum, Asian Pacific American Forum, Hispanic Forum, Women's Network, and Veteran's Network. There are also numerous employee groups that the company supports in the GE businesses, the largest of which is the Gay, Lesbian, Bisexual, Transgender and Allies (GLBTA) Alliance.

In addition, GE established their Corporate Diversity Council (CDC) as a way to engage the most senior business and functional leaders across the company. Co-chaired by GE's Chairman and CEO with the Chief Diversity Officer, the CDC meets quarterly to discuss diversity strategies and ideas, review primary initiatives and monitor progress. The CDC also takes a deep-dive into business diversity initiatives, challenges and opportunities. Through discussions in these meetings, the CDC leverages the affinity networks to support and accelerate key company initiatives. For example, when the Healthymagination initiative was rolled out, GE's Asian Pacific American Forum (APAF) spread the word and collaborated on specific projects with the businesses. Because of its success at the company level, this CDC model has been replicated across GE's sub-businesses around the globe and used for business level diversity strategy discussions.

Maryam Hameed, an engineer at GE Healthcare, helps Igniting Minds students from Morse Middle School in Milwaukee, Wisconsin, learn about science, technology, engineering, and mathematics (STEM)

The contributions of APAF employees have been recognized by reputed external organizations such as Asia Society, ASCEND and SASE. The forum is led by three national champions and sponsored by two senior executives. The executive sponsors are Senior Vice Presidents from the Chairman's senior management staff. Programs and events are aligned to three areas: (1) helping members, (2) helping the community and (3) helping the company, and include training workshops, networking sessions, speaker events, talent roundtables, community service events and cultural celebrations. One such program is Igniting Minds™.

With the U.S. falling behind the world in math and science proficiency standings, APAF developed Igniting Minds, a program targeted towards improving students' confidence in these subject areas and fostering interest in pursuing science, technology, engineering or math careers (STEM careers). The program is a 15-week, volunteer-based program where GE employees teach concept-based lesson plans to students in public middle schools in underserved communities. The curriculum is designed to teach math and science fundamentals, aligned to core standards, and is delivered in a fun, interactive, real-life application activity. Igniting Minds™ is currently offered in thirteen schools in nine states. The program has received recognition including an award from Public Education Partners as making a difference in school's proficiency standings.

 The single most significant driver of diversity and inclusion at **Merck** is Chief Executive Officer, Kenneth Frazier, who drives this commitment throughout all ranks of Merck globally. He ensures that the Merck vision incorporates diversity; signs off on executive compensation tied to diversity; approves and reviews progress against stated goals; meets with senior leaders throughout the year to review key strategic initiatives; and approves goals and reviews achievements for supplier diversity. Externally, Mr. Frazier is a highly sought after speaker on several topics. He was asked to speak on the core ideals of diversity and inclusion and their critical importance in the global business community at the JKF50: Justice for All event, "Leading with Diversity in a Global Economy."

> Kenneth Frasier, CEO, Merck: *"I am puzzled why we ask about bottom line impact of diversity when we do not ask about the impact of homogeneity. We know imagination and creativity require bringing together diverse perspectives."*

Merck is advancing its GD&I mission in 2012 with the creation of the Business Insight Roundtable (BIR). The BIR, comprised of nine groups—Asia Pacific, African Ancestry, Differently Able, Hispanic, Interfaith, LGBT, Native American, Women and Veteran—will focus on critical GD&I priorities, such as: delivering leadership training and development to our global employee constituents; identifying diverse high-potential talent; obtaining business insights to help franchise leaders drive effective decision-making on growth opportunities; and, partnering with community and strategic organizations to enhance our image and reputation as a responsible global corporate citizen. Over 6,000 Merck employees are members of the nine ERGs, which are now aligned to the Roundtable and working on the priorities identified by BIR areas of focus.

Merck Asia Pacific Network developed and executed a number of programs that benefit APA employees and the firm as a whole. The Annual APA Summit featured Peter Kim, President, Merck Research Laboratories as the keynote speaker as well as a distinguished panel of Merck leaders. A training module entitled "The Art of Cultural Fluency: Bridging Asian and Western

Leadership Styles," in collaboration with Jane Hyun and Associates, contained exercises to reinforce learning, learning tests and final assessment, and a summary report, upon completion of the module for future reference.

From a global perspective the ERGs have created five Briefing Books (Brazil, China, India, Israel and Mexico) to help Merck employees who are planning to visit and do business in these markets, by providing key knowledge on health care needs, cultural nuances, and business etiquette required to host successful meetings with global partners. These Briefing Books are available on Merck's internal website and are also complimented by a video on cultural best practices by country. The "A Spotlight on Culture" video clips share valuable global insights that help to build an understanding of the business landscape for vaccines throughout the world.

CP **COLGATE-PALMOLIVE** COMPANY **Colgate-Palmolive Company** ensures that people have the ability to relate to each other regardless of their diverse backgrounds. Their Fostering an Inclusive Work Environment (FIWE) program provides a broad awareness of diversity and incorporates key diversity skills and tools into every team member's day-to-day responsibilities to include coaching for performance, valuing unique contributions, communicating effectively, giving and receiving feedback and promoting teamwork.

The Employee Resource Groups (ERGs) support Colgate-Palmolive's strategic initiatives of Engage to Build our Brands, Effectiveness and Efficiency, Innovation for Growth, and Leading to Win by building an inclusive and caring work environment. The ERGs support initiatives to attract, develop, and retain a diverse workforce. These associations provide excellent opportunities for networking, mentoring and leadership development.

The Asian Action Network's (AAN) mission is to foster an environment of caring and global teamwork by valuing cultural diversity through programs that celebrate the richness of Asian cultures. Through AAN Colgate-Palmolive people of Asian descent can maximize their full potential and contribute to the Colgate-Palmolive business. The Colgate-Palmolive Country Series sponsored by AAN and presented each quarter by key business leaders provides an opportunity to learn how Asian subsidiaries contribute to business building. This allows APA employees the opportunity to have a tangible impact on the business, as these sessions enable Colgate-Palmolive headquarters to better support the subsidiaries in growing their business.

A hallmark of Colgate-Palmolive's network programs is the impetus to collaborate across groups. AAN and the GLBT network sponsored the Asia Society's network mixer attended by 300 professionals to build leadership skills and grow professional networks. Since 2008, Colgate-Palmolive has sponsored the Cross-Cultural Women's Symposium developed by Madrinas and the Asian Women Leadership Network (AWLN). In 2010, AAN and the Hispanic Action Network introduced, an executive leader interview: Inside the Leader's Studio, The Person Behind the Leader, where executives shared insights on leadership skills for success at Colgate-Palmolive. The networks really value this and feel that their work is enriched when they can do programming together.

Goldman Sachs **Goldman Sachs** supports over 80 affinity networks and interest forums globally. The networks are open to all employees and engage everyone at the firm in fostering an inclusive work environment and complement the company's broader diversity and inclusion strategy. The Asian Professionals Network (APN) was launched in October 2001 and is comprised of nine divisional and two regional Asian professionals' networks that function to complement the work of the larger firm wide network through more nuanced offerings that cater to the needs of the divisional populations. In 2011, membership in the Asian Professionals Networks (APN) increased by 30 percent.

A year-long, qualitative research study with more than 100 professionals and members of Goldman Sachs' Asian Professionals Network in every region and across all divisions resulted in the creation of a new training initiative titled "Voices from Asia: Redefining Global Leadership." A collaboration between Goldman Sachs University, the Office of Global Leadership and Diversity and the APN, the initiative utilizes an interactive approach to educate participants on the wide spectrum of Asian professionals working at the firm. Training materials include "Voices from Goldman Sachs: Perspectives from Your Colleagues," that highlights testimonials from global colleagues sharing how culture influences their approach to work and provides advice on how to "flex" one's style. The Center for Work-Life Policy highlighted the initiative as a best practice in their research report, "Asians in America: Unleashing the Potential of the Model Minority," which Goldman Sachs sponsored.

> Senior Manager, Goldman Sachs:
> *"In order to affect change and impact the professional development of Asian professionals at the firm, it was not enough to offer leadership and management-related training to Asians—we had to raise awareness and educate a wider audience, including managers and co-workers across the firm."*

The affinity networks also host a number of professional development programs for their members throughout the year focused on crucial career development topics. For example, the Human Capital Management APN hosted a signature event on "Raising Your Profile" facilitated by the Americas head of the internal leadership development group Pine Street, and featuring senior Asian professionals in the division sharing best practices.

APN also organizes a full calendar of events celebrating Asian Pacific American Heritage Month (APAHM). 2011 celebrations of APAHM were marked by record levels of engagement; over 1,000 network members participated in heritage month events throughout offices in the Americas.

 IBM has over 250 Diversity Network Groups, of which 23 are Asian Pacific American. This is an opportunity for the constituency to network, participate in community outreach programs and professional and market development. In 1995, IBM commissioned eight diversity task forces to develop recommendations to ensure their constituents felt welcomed and valued as members of Team IBM, maximize their productivity, and maximize the relationship of IBM with their constituents in the marketplace. These task forces, focusing on Asian, Black, Gay/Lesbian, Hispanic/Latino, Native American, People with Disabilities, Men, and Women, recommended instituting Diversity Network Groups as a tool to help achieve IBM business objectives. These groups consist of IBM employees who voluntarily come together with the ultimate goal of enhancing the success of IBM's business objectives by helping their members become more effective in the workplace through: networking; mentoring and coaching; community outreach; planning and implementing social; cultural and educational events; developing professional skills; enhancing recruitment and welcoming, and sharing information.

IBM offers employees the opportunity to create communities of interest, for example: Women in Technology, Other than Traditional Office, Sports, Cultural, etc.

Diversity Councils have been created to increase the focus on local or unique diversity issues. Through these councils, IBM ensures that its workforce represents an environment that visibly encourages and values the contributions and differences of employees from various backgrounds. IBM's Asian Executive Council consists of three vice presidents, who are the co-chairs, and two senior vice presidents. Focus areas consist of leadership, pipeline and collaboration. They developed a first-of-its-kind Asian Annual Report that is shared with all U.S. Asian employees. It highlights APA employees who are making a difference in the community, external partnerships, awards and recognition, and commitment from executives. This model is now a major part of how all Diversity Network groups communicate.

Diversity Training is required for all of IBM. Training is offered both internally and externally, and can be virtual or face-to-face. Metrics are in place to assess the diversity training and specific programs offered to new employees and managers. Examples of training programs include: Inclusive Leadership for Managers: Leading in a Diverse Environment, Inclusion in the Workplace for Employees, Becoming an Inclusive IBM Leader, MicroInequities: The Power of Small, Work Life Flexibility for Managers and Employees, Shades of Blue for Employees.

Recruitment and Selection

This dimension had some of the strongest programs. Best practices integrate employee resource group members, senior management and HR professionals within a seamless framework. The focus was not on specific quotas but rather aligning business objectives with the need to increase the number of diverse candidates in the pipeline. Companies have found value in having relationships with external APA organizations, both as a source of recruits and more importantly, as a source of programming to address the recruiting issues internally.

 New York Life Insurance Company undertakes a biannual employee survey. The information from the survey allows the company to develop programs to address the issues and opportunities identified from the survey within targeted employee populations. For example, New York Life's Career Management Initiative was launched as a development experience designed to strengthen the career advancement and engagement of mid-level professionals from historically underrepresented groups. Over the course of four months, the program focuses on three key themes—Career Development, Business Acumen and Leadership. The goal of the program is for the participants to better understand the key factors for career success and to develop strategies for building confidence and critical professional relationships.

In order to increase and maintain the number of minority and female candidates for management positions within New York Life, the Executive Management Committee, which is comprised of New York Life's senior executive leadership and assists the CEO in setting policy for the company, has mandated that for mid-level and executive positions, minority and female candidates with the requisite skills be interviewed. The applicant pool requirement is monitored and recorded on a monthly basis within New York Life's Office of Diversity & Inclusion.

The company also undertakes a quarterly review of its employee population to ensure that they are maintaining and/or improving representation of all minority groups in the organization, including Asian Pacific American employees. There is a semiannual promotion cycle during which the company carefully monitors and reviews all candidates being considered for promotion. A close collaboration among Human Resources business partners, departmental diversity officers, and senior leaders within each business unit ensures full consideration has been given to all candidates for promotion in each cycle.

Freddie Mac has forged strong partnerships within the Asian Pacific American community and across professional external organizations, such as ASCEND. These relationships have helped to generate a strong pipeline of top talent to the company and provided effective development programs to help retain and advance the careers of this talent within the organization. The talent acquisition process incorporates best practices in outreach and recruiting to enhance the diversity of the candidate pools from which hiring occurs. Further supporting the company's commitment to recruit and retain diverse talent, educational programs are presented to HR Recruiters and Business Division Hiring Managers to enhance their cross-cultural competency and explore the personal filters which they may apply in the review, interview and selection process of employee candidates. These programs, "Enhancing Your Cultural Competency" and "Recruiting through a Diversity Lens," are two workshops that are highly valued across the businesses within the company and have been embedded as a requirement in many of their customized business diversity & inclusion plans.

Additionally, in some cases Freddie Mac uses a diverse panel of interviewers to conduct candidate interviews. These efforts provide the opportunity for additional perspectives and considerations to be offered in the candidate assessment and evaluation process.

The Employee Network Ambassador program has focused on training selected members from the seven employee network groups on best practices for representing Freddie Mac at diverse external job/career fairs, conferences and seminars. This program provides the opportunity for external candidates exploring the company as a potential employer to meet and speak directly with a Freddie Mac employee of their same identity group. This also serves as a highly effective recruiting mechanism for the networks themselves, if the recruit becomes an employee at the firm. Ambassadors are trained to share their candid personal and professional perspectives of the company's benefits, development programs, environment, opportunities, etc. A philosophy of 'no spin' has contributed to Freddie Mac's ability to attract top diverse talent.

> Suzanne Richards, Vice President, Diversity & Inclusion, Freddie Mac: *"We don't want any barriers to finding the right people."*

The Ambassador program is being expanded to include representatives from the company's business divisions, in addition to the employee network members, due to its success and the value that the businesses and the employees derive from it.

Using the **Merck** Corporate Scorecard to track representation of diverse employees, Merck ensures that the candidate selection process is inclusive of diversity goals. In addition, the company partners with organizations in both professional as well as academic settings to net the company a more diverse mix of capable talent.

Several recruiting and outreach initiatives seek and attract a diverse candidate pool. Merck uses a comprehensive, 360-degree approach to ensure its recruiting, retention, and leadership development goals are systematically executed throughout the organization. Beyond standard recruiting best practices, the company has expanded its use of new technology media to reach prospective candidates with the Merck story. Examples include the creation of diversity career videos (www.careertv.com) and the Merck Careers group in Facebook, a key tool to attract interns to the company and also make visible current job opportunities in different divisions.

Merck uses targeted recruiting materials and brochures to ensure that it communicates its mission and vision to prospective candidates. Leaders from the company who are of Asian heritage are leveraged to speak at various university and college settings to provide real-life examples and testimonials of the career track one can achieve at Merck. Utilizing senior leaders also provides an opportunity for students and employee candidates to network and learn more about specific functional areas in which they have an interest.

The Merck Asian Employee Resource Group, the Asia Pacific Association (APA), also plays an important role in supporting the diversity outreach efforts for Merck and in providing recommendations and referrals to high quality talent. Seminars and events are held throughout the year to promote Merck as employer of choice among candidates in the biosciences, medical and chemical engineering fields, among others.

IBM focuses on the recruitment of a diverse workforce with a primary interest in top talent. The wide array of recruitment sources IBM uses has been very successful in attracting a large number of Asian Pacific American candidates. The campus recruiting program in the U.S. is broad and covers many colleges throughout the 50 states and includes candidates from the University of Hawaii. There is a strong focus on campus by the IBM Recruiting Team to collaborate with diversity student organizations and many candidates are sourced as a result of these relationships. For more than 30 years IBM has supported diversity programs such as Inroads, GEM, CGSM and Entry Point that promote academic excellence as well as organizations that provide funding for minorities and women. IBM has a robust internship program that provides students with an industry experience and exposes them to real world business and technology solutions. IBM was selected as the company of the year in 2010 at the first National Asian MBAs conference held in NYC. IBM has also been a strong supporter of the National Association of Asian American Professionals (NA@AP).

IBM has several home-grown programs that attract talented Asian Pacific Americans, such as the 22-year-old Project View program. In 2005 Project View was recognized by the OFCCP with the Freedom to Compete award as a Best Practice. Project View is a recruiting channel created by IBM as a recruitment program that focuses on women and underrepresented minority top talent. The program also enables candidates to meet with representatives, not only from HR and recruiting, but also from the businesses who can provide specific details and real-life experience about the positions. IBM managers who attend Project View are authorized to offer a position on the spot and the programs are specifically targeted to areas where IBM can expect a large pool of talented diverse candidates. This allows IBM to better recruit the best diverse candidates, who are often the very first to receive job offers.

KPMG is committed to attracting and retaining a diverse workforce. The Future Diversity Leaders program offers scholarships and internship opportunities each year to 50-65 high-achieving ethnically diverse students, including Asian Pacific Americans. Students must demonstrate a strong academic performance, leadership skills, and a commitment to diversity. The program encourages students to consider pursuing a career in business, while preparing those same high-potential students to be the business leaders of tomorrow. Those who successfully complete their internship and maintain a high academic standing are offered a full-time position with KPMG.

APIN (KPMG's APA employee network) supports local campus recruiting efforts in many offices by hosting events and networking with prospects. For example, APIN members in Chicago hosted the ASCEND Student Leadership Conference, which provided opportunities to develop relationships with local college students. Members of the company's Washington, D.C./Tysons Corner APIN chapter organized a networking event designed to help KPMG interns better get to know the firm, its resources, and employer of choice initiatives.

KPMG's relationship with ASCEND offers additional ways for the firm to get to know, and potentially recruit, high-performing Asian Pacific American students. For the second consecutive year, KPMG sponsored the ASCEND National Case Study Competition at September's ASCEND National Conference. The competition involves college accounting students solving real-life accounting issues, and KPMG professionals advise students as they manage their way through the exercise.

From an infrastructure perspective, the firm created the Recruiting Champion role, designating one person from each network chapter to collaborate with the firm's recruiting team to ensure that the firm has a diverse population of employees involved in its campus recruiting process. KPMG's Experienced Hire Recruiting organization includes a team of professionals focused on diversity recruiting strategies and initiatives. In addition, the Senior Talent Acquisition initiative addresses KPMG's core hiring needs and helps accelerate the representation of female and ethnic minorities in the partnership. The firm's Diversity Advisory Board Scorecard was developed to set meaningful diversity metrics for the firm. It comprises a core set of diversity metrics addressing headcount, promotions, retention, and mentoring.

Another strong retention tool is a highly-focused communication program. For example, as KPMG executes its "go-to-market" strategy, it is crucial that market development leaders communicate regularly with all employees, not only to promote understanding around the strategy, but also to build confidence that the firm has the right leadership team in place. Accordingly, KPMG's Vice Chair for Market Strategy, and one of KPMG's National Managing Partners, have had a high profile in the firm's communications programs. They are frequent in-person speakers at KPMG offices where they discuss the "go-to-market" strategy with partners and employees, and they are often featured in articles in KPMG Today, the firm's intranet and news site, through messages they write themselves as well as stories in which they are quoted.

 GE's Corporate Diversity Council, led by GE's Chairman and CEO, tracks and reviews the retention and attrition of diverse talent, including APAs during their quarterly meetings. GE has a variety of leadership development programs, which serve as both recruiting and training programs, e.g., the human resources leadership program, information management leadership program, operations management leadership program, commercial leadership program and financial management leadership program. GE attracts exceptional talent from all backgrounds and focuses on recruiting diverse talent into those programs. Members of APAF (GE's APA employee resource group) also actively participate in on-campus recruiting efforts that support this process.

The Early Identification (EID) is the primary pipeline of talent into the leadership development programs, as well as into hundreds of direct hire positions. Racial/Ethnic diversity of the EID populations is over 33 percent. The company also actively recruits at seven major diversity student organizations: Society of Asian Scientists and Engineers (SASE), Society of Women Engineers (SWE), National Society of Black Engineers (NSBE), Society of Hispanic Professional Engineers (SHPE), National Society of Hispanic MBAs (NSHMBA), National Black MBA Association (NBMBAA) and American Indian Science and Engineering Society (AISES). EID program interns and co-ops exceeded 3,000 in 2011. Maintaining existing and building new external connections at top collegiate schools and organizations was another area of focus for APAF. These relationships have increased the goodwill of GE with future graduates and strengthened the pipeline for recruitment opportunities.

GE's partnership with student organizations encompasses integrated strategic programming. For example, for the past two years, GE has been a member of the Society of Asian Scientists and Engineers (SASE). Chapters in top colleges and universities around the country help prepare APA student members for science and engineering careers, celebrate diversity on campuses and in the workplace, provide opportunities for community service and provide a forum for recruitment. Through GE's APAF's support, 13 chapters at colleges across the U.S. have been launched, with another four in progress. GE's "Point of Contacts" have engaged and connected the SASE chapters with GE corporate recruiting teams for engineering co-ops/internships and permanent hire opportunities in U.S. and China. In addition, GE Aviation has hired 10 SASE students for 2011 summer co-op positions. This commitment will continue at GE Aviation each year.

Retention Efforts

Much like its recruiting counterpart, best practices along the Retention dimension demonstrate a wide array of approaches. But commonalities include alignment with professional development, rewards and recognition and again, an integral role for employee networks. Whether the programs were developed wholly within the organization, or were the product of relationships with external APA associations, these companies have all prioritized overall employee engagement as the best way to increasing retention.

Goldman Sachs

Goldman Sachs has further expanded its diversity efforts to respond to the ever-evolving needs of its diverse professionals, positively impacting retention, building loyalty, and increasing cultural awareness throughout the firm. The Office of Global Leadership and Diversity and Goldman Sachs University sponsor various programs to strengthen the engagement and retention of diverse talent. These programs often consist of high-impact events designed to provide visible role models, promote commercial development, encourage networking, and comprehensively acknowledge the issues that can affect individuals at various points throughout their career life-cycle.

In 2011, the firm launched "Voices from Asia: Redefining Global Leadership" an innovative program focused on the workplace experience of Asian professionals. By exploring how cultural values impact the workplace and gaining a better understanding of the workplace experience of Asian colleagues, participants expand their perceptions of effective leadership and communication and learn best practices to maximize the potential of global talent.

Participant, Redefining Global Leadership: *"The program has great potential to educate, sensitize and to a certain extent demystify complexities"* one participant commented.

Before the formal launch of the program, three pilot sessions were held and feedback has been overwhelmingly positive. 96 percent of participants responded that the program helped them better understand the diversity of Asian cultures and recognize how culture influences communication style, meeting facilitation, building relationships, management style and self-promotion. In December 2011, Goldman Sachs held the first follow-up session to the program with a roundtable discussion hosted by the head of the Federation divisions in Asia. Since the official launch of "Voices from Asia" in November, over 250 managers have completed the course and feedback continues to be extremely positive.

 IBM's Asian Executive Council continues to remain active throughout the U.S. Their objectives are to 1) recommend and advocate policies and practices as well as provide leadership for their constituency, 2) create an atmosphere where employees are valued and personal productivity and effectiveness are maximized, 3) attract, develop and retain talent, 4) drive increased revenue and market share globally. The council focuses on developing their constituency and bringing awareness to the community that will grow them personally and professionally, for example, panel discussions, mentor programs, F2F roundtable discussions, and recognizing holidays that celebrate food, culture and experiences for everyone to learn, etc.

In addition, IBM has employee-driven groups called Diversity Network Groups. Asian Diversity Network Groups are grassroots efforts led by employees who are passionate about helping other Asian employees succeed and become role models for incoming talent. IBM is constantly making sure they are building their pipeline and making an impact. They host activities that educate and bring awareness to the broader IBM community. This allows them to interact and network with executives that lead mentoring opportunities that can help them grow their career goals. There are 23 Asian Diversity Network Groups registred in the U.S.; however, there are possibly many more as registration of a group is not required.

Ron Glover, Chief Diversity Officer, IBM: *"All the communities that IBM is creating are a way to make sure that employees feel valued and that we build within our organization the capacity to work and succeed across differences."*

Formal diversity metrics associated with the succession planning program are tracked. On a monthly basis, IBM tracks promotions and external hires of women and minorities into executive positions against a placement rate target established for each executive level. The placement rate targets are established at the beginning of each year by IBM's Diversity Organization and are identical to those included in IBM's Affirmative Action Program, which is provided to the U.S. Government. This placement rate is the estimated rate at which women and minorities, through promotions and external hires, are expected to be placed into executive levels. The rates are based on a weighted calculation of internal and external percentages of promotable women and minorities. The annual total retention rate for the Asian constituency is 88.2 percent for men and women.

Freddie Mac's efforts to retain top talent at the organization focus on all demographic groups. Throughout the year, the company monitors voluntary and involuntary attrition rates across all groups. Where necessary, this is followed by "spot" or "climate" surveys to help better understand and address areas where significant variations in attrition rates may exist.

While retention rates among Asian Pacific Americans and other Asian employees typically score highest across demographic groups, Freddie Mac believes it is just as important that the engagement levels of these employees, and all employees, remain positive, via research to determine employee satisfaction, measurement and comparative analysis of the company's engagement survey results across all demographic groups, including ethnic groups, gender, and position level. This more detailed breakdown allows the company to develop programs and practices that address identified concerns that may be raised by specific employee segments. Flexibility was one such issue. In response to concerns expressed in the engagement survey, Freddie Mac's Human Resources Department, working in conjunction with the D&I department and the employee resource groups, developed a flexible work arrangement program which was rolled out leveraging senior level communications and the employee resource groups. Tracking of survey responses has shown a great improvement on this dimension, especially as employees recognize that an issue that was raised in the survey was directly addressed.

Other programs that contribute to high retention across their diverse workforce include the seven employee networks, and the Ambassador Programs. Ambassadors help to attract top talent to the organization but also play an important role in employee retention. Within the first week of employment, employees are introduced to the seven employee network groups and invited to participate in their initiatives. Shortly thereafter, an employee network Ambassador schedules a one-on-one meeting with the employee to share more information about the network groups, diversity and inclusion programs, and other information that will support new hires as they acclimatize to their new role and the company. Within 90 days of employment, employees must complete an online diversity module, which reinforces Freddie Mac's focus on a diverse and inclusive working environment, highlights available communication channels, and provides details on how to engage in diversity related initiatives. After 90 days of employment, employees are provided a survey to complete, which focuses on their on-boarding experience, as well as engagement in diversity/employee network initiatives.

KPMG is committed to helping all professionals develop personally and professionally. Programs and initiatives such as professional learning and development, Employee Career Architecture, Global Mobility program, and others are designed to ensure people have multiple avenues for improving their skills and building their careers.

KPMG developed the People Management Leader (PML) program because research across all demographic groups showed that a major reason that people leave, or remain with, their organization is their direct supervisor. Through the program, people management responsibilities are in the hands of a smaller group of well-trained, senior-level professionals who have proven their ability to guide the careers and manage the performance of others. To support the process and the PMLs, new resources are continually developed to enhance existing offerings. These include PML Alerts and a PML Dashboard, which provide timely information to each PML about their direct reports and important action items. A comprehensive web site centralizes the information the PMLs need.

Diversity networks, including APIN (KPMG's APA employee resource group), play an important role in furthering professional development and retention. For example, Houston's APIN chapter sponsored and hosted ASCEND's "Inspiring Across Generations" conference. In Chicago, APIN members attended the Corporate Leadership Conference, sponsored by KPMG and 11 other companies in the city; the half-day event focused on personal and professional leadership development.

In addition, the APIN Professional Development and Mentoring Subcommittee distributed a curriculum of web-based soft skills courses to all local APIN chapters to use as developmental opportunities with their members. This resulted from the firm's analysis that indicated turnover among Asian Pacific Americans increased at the "senior associate" level due to their concerns that their relative lack of essential soft skills might inhibit their career growth. Training includes topics such as how to make an impact in the boardroom, public speaking and relationship development.

 **COLGATE-PALMOLIVE** COMPANY **Colgate-Palmolive** strives to be an employer of choice by providing stimulating careers that provide training, education, and growth opportunities; creating an exciting and motivating work environment; ensuring that people feel recognized and rewarded; promoting fundamental values and ongoing communication that keeps people feeling connected; supporting activities and accomplishments that reflect the corporate values of Caring, Global Teamwork and Continuous Improvement; ensuring a feeling of belonging by recruiting and retaining people of all backgrounds in its global workforce; encouraging a healthy balance between work and personal responsibilities.

To foster an environment of trust, community and open communication, the company has established a Managing with Respect philosophy. All Colgate-Palmolive people are responsible for practicing the five principles of Managing with Respect: Communicating Effectively; Giving and Seeking Feedback; Valuing Unique Contributions; Promoting Teamwork; Setting the Example. Every manager receives a grade on each component and an overall grade. Unsatisfactory scores have a direct affect on compensation.

> Eugene Kelly, Chief Diversity Officer: *"The company really wants performance, but it's important that these results are achieved in a respectful and inclusive manner; and everyone regardless of level is held accountable. Though someone may achieve strong business results in the short-term, we recognize that without respectful management, there is a negative impact on the company and its people.*

The recruiting, training, promotion and retention of women and minorities are built into the managerial bonus structure. The Chairman, President & CEO of the company direct this initiative. Individual management efforts in promoting women and minorities into key leadership positions are included in managerial objectives and performance evaluations. A critical piece of the retention strategy is to ensure that Colgate-Palmolive's Global Succession Planning process incorporates a component that further reviews the professional development of women and minorities. The company's senior-most executives participate in these conversations to develop action plans to further develop women and minorities and set specific targets by organization based on labor force availability. In addition, each organization is expected to report periodically on progress toward reaching these diversity targets.

GE's Corporate Diversity Council reviews retention of diverse talent and key metrics, including voluntary attrition, on a quarterly basis. This is also monitored by each business and actions are put in place based on need. For example, GE Capital has focused considerable attention on retention because of the significant turmoil in financial services over the past few years. The business held a national symposium last November with APAF (GE's APA employee resource group), with representation of 80 engaged members from 10 chapter/hubs across GE Capital and their business CEO & President.

Rewards and recognition are core components. GE's Affinity Networks hold National Meetings where high-performers are nominated to attend. During these meetings, participants are exposed to senior leaders, notable speakers, cutting-edge workshops and industry experts. Growth Leadership and Hub Awards are presented to APAs who demonstrated functional expertise, embody the GE values and have contributed back to the company and APAF.

GE Chairman Jeffrey Immelt, APAF leaders, and the National Meeting organizing team at the 2012 APAF National Meeting in Washington, DC.

APAF has within its structure 11 Business Liaisons, held by senior-level APAs, who serve as the conduit between APAF and the GE businesses. Business Liaisons are highly visible roles, participating in each business's Diversity Council, annual employee review process (Session C) and diversity strategy planning. They help to elevate the visibility of APAs within their business, driving retention and engagement amongst its members.

APAF also periodically surveys its members to gain feedback and validate areas to develop and engage and where focus may be needed. For example, APAF has been working closely with the APA female population to identify specific needs and challenges. This led to the launch of the APA Women initiative and programs such as the APA Women Speaker Series, which provides topics relevant to this population including Success under Stress, Managing Conflict, and Building Your Power Base.

APAF distributes a quarterly coast-to-coast newsletter to maintain connections and recognize their efforts. Messages from APAF National Leaders, highlights on hub activities and events, progress on APAF and GE initiatives, and celebrations of APA promotions and achievements are communicated, providing an effective touch point to employees. Across its various national digital media touch points, APAF has reached close to 30,000 hits showcasing its commitment to connecting to employees with timely and impactful communications. Providing opportunities to connect and engage employees is core to APAF's retention strategy, with more than 350 events in 2011 including training workshops, networking sessions, speaker events, talent roundtables, community service, and cultural events. Members are also able to build leadership skills by organizing, leading and participating in APAF events. Additionally, the APAF Leadership Council has been meeting with the membership across the country to help foster retention.

Members of APAF's Northern California hub sorted over 42,000 pounds of fruit for the San Francisco Food Bank in 2011

Employee Growth & Advancement

APA survey results show that employees truly value professional growth and development, and yet overall this dimension is scored the least favorably from year to year. The programs in this section demonstrate an approach that goes beyond general training and instead focuses on the development of tools and resources, personalization/customization and tracking and measurement as key components of professional development programs overall. Many of the programs are for all employees, demonstrating that a company does not have to have specific APA programs to successfully impact their APA employees' growth and development.

CORNING Growth and development are ingrained in the daily activities at **Corning**. Employees are provided with the keys to success beginning with the new employee on-boarding process called Become Corning and the career planning tool My Development. Become Corning is a series of learning and information modules for new employees within their first six months, which includes modules on diversity and the value of the Affinity Groups. Much is made of the value of the groups and how they serve as a way for professional development.

The My Development program takes over for an employee's first one to three years at Corning, allowing employees to develop career paths, set goals and again highlighting affinity group participation and leadership as key ways to advance their careers through networking, professional development and leadership development. My Development assists employees by providing tools and information to facilitate career exploration, assessment against desired competencies and behaviors and design of robust and targeted development plans and guided learning. The Global Diversity office sponsors the Efficacy of Leadership training targeting current and emerging leaders of the affinity groups. Participants assess their skills through a comprehensive 360 analysis and develop personal goals. The attendees set goals and complete strategic planning for their affinity group.

Affinity groups offer career development training or coaching programs. For example Corning's Chinese Association hosts events for skills development and sponsors the Corning Chinese School & Chemung Chinese School. Volunteers from the APA community run the Chinese School. The company has many courses for supervisors, such as Dimensions of Leadership and Supervisor Effectiveness, which have diversity & inclusion pieces in the curriculum. There are also classroom and experiential learning opportunities for supervisors.

While these programs are for all employees, Corning's APA employees have definitely benefited as their high participation in affinity groups demonstrates. For example, an APA employee who was on an expat assignment in China mentioned to the diversity officer that the training on leadership development and diversity she gained as an AG leader and also via the career development modules really helped her succeed in the new environment. Even though she was of Chinese descent, she recognized that her perspective was different as an Asian Pacific American and was able to adapt accordingly.

Freddie Mac offers a robust suite of programs to develop employee management and leadership skills. Freddie Mac University (FMU) offers dozens of both self-paced online and instructor-led courses that are available for open enrollment to all Freddie Mac employees. The company has created 'learning tracts,' certificate programs, and elective offerings for specific topics such as leadership, management, technical, self-development, communication, diversity, etc. Training and development is incorporated as a part of each employee's individual development plan and performance assessment. This practice ensures each employee has at least three annual one-on-one meetings with their managers to discuss their personal and professional development goals, needs, and actions. Employees are supported financially by Freddie Mac to enhance their education via participation in external programs, seminars, colleges and universities.

In 2010, Freddie Mac also launched an 'in-house' MS in Finance program, taught by the American University of Washington DC. Participants represent the diversity of the organization (27 percent of the initial cohort are Asian Pacific American employees) and this program supports efforts to develop the leaders of today and tomorrow. The company's most recent program, Master of Professional Studies in Technology Management, will also support these efforts. To educate employees about the unique challenges that may confront Asian Pacific American employees in their career aspirations, Freddie Mac annually invites prominent Asian American speakers to share the challenges and successes they have experienced in their careers. Recent speakers include Tammy Duckworth, Assistant Secretary of the United States Department of Veteran Affairs, and renowned diversity consultant and educator, Dr. Steve Robbins, on his unique approach to understanding and benefiting from workplace diversity.

The firm's Enhancing Your Cultural Competency workshop is available to all employees and is designed to increase cultural awareness and improve meaningful communication, which in turn helps to support diverse employees in their professional advancement and growth. There is also a career development program tailored for Asian Pacific American employees. This includes a full day, self-efficacy workshop for Asian Americans titled "Asian American Leadership in the 21st Century."

Through partnerships with external organizations, the company is also able to offer career development opportunities via conferences, seminars, leadership positions, etc. In 2011, partnerships providing opportunities for APA employees included Ascend Pan-Asian Leaders, the Asia Society, the American Society of Women Accountants, and the National Association of Professional Mortgage Women. Participation in such partnerships and available programs are being embedded into many of the business division Diversity & Inclusion plans.

 **KPMG**'s High-Performance Culture Initiative was launched in 2011 to help the firm and its people succeed in today's environment—one that is always evolving, always moving forward, and always demanding more. This means finding ways to take performance to "the next level." Kicked off via a web-based primer for all partners and employees called "The Next Level," the initiative is reinforced through additional training, resources, enhanced performance management, and more. According to KPMG's most recent firm-wide employee survey, the High-Performance Culture Initiative is resonating with Asian Pacific American employees. Those who agree that the firm is "taking it to the next level" are more likely to feel high engagement with the organization.

KPMG offers employees abundant opportunities to enrich their skills and advance their careers. The firm offers a comprehensive lifecycle curriculum of training programs that focus on functional expertise, professional credentials, enhancing personal effectiveness and business acumen, building leadership, and strategic thinking. In fiscal year 2011, there were more than 5,200 sessions of 2,769 instructor-led courses, plus 1,649 e-learning courses, enabling employees to collectively earn almost 1.4 million Continuing Professional Education credits.

The firm's Diversity Networks also are a major resource for learning and development, providing participants with networking and skill-building opportunities. Network members from the firm's Asian Pacific Islander Network (APIN) are among attendees of the KPMG Executive Institute for Women, a quarterly forum designed to provide practical instruction in leadership development for women who have already achieved a high level of success. KPMG also sponsors one high-performing senior manager/director, managing director, or partner each year to attend Stanford University's Advanced Leadership Program for Asian American Executives (designed to accelerate the development of global business skills).

Kathy Hannan, KPMG's National Managing Partner, Diversity and Corporate Responsibility, and chair of the firm's Diversity Advisory Board (DAB), works with business leaders on identifying and evaluating diverse candidates from the company's functional pipelines, to help better understand and support their specific development needs. The company's Leaders Engaging Leaders career advising program establishes one-to-one mentoring relationships between members of KPMG 's Board of Directors and Management Committee and high-performing diverse partners, including Asian Pacific Americans. KPMG's U.S. Global Mobility program provides all professionals with opportunities to take developmental assignments in KPMG International member firms around the world. Currently, 85 professionals from the KPMG U.S. member firm are on temporary assignments at KPMG member firms in the Asia Pacific region.

 **Merck** offers a wide range of training and educational programs and resources to create a transformative organization and stimulate employees to achieve their full potential.

Merck sponsors a skills development curriculum to build leadership and management skills for all levels of employees globally. "The Art of Cultural Fluency: Bridging Asian and Western Leadership Styles," a new, one-hour online cultural training module, contains video segments with Jane Hyun, author of Breaking the Bamboo Ceiling; interactive exercises to reinforce learning; three learning tests and one final assessment; and, a summary report upon completion of module for future reference. It is open to all employees. The company's iLead site houses approximately 5,000 - 6,000 learning resources that employees can use to develop their leadership skills at all levels. Resources are available in the following formats: "on demand" web-based modules, classroom, on-the-job development suggestions, articles, and video podcasts.

There is also a suite of programs for team development and team building that range from formal learning experiences to "action learning"- based interventions that help teams develop skills and competencies as they pursue real business goals. For those earlier in their career, the You & Your Success program aims to help employees manage their careers and align personal and professional objectives with practical strategies for achieving both.

Merck Sigma, based on the six-sigma approach, is designed to maximize efficiency, reduce errors and minimize risks. Merck conducts regular Lean Six Sigma training for employees, which leads to "Green Belt," "Black Belt" and "Executive Belt" certification in Merck Sigma tools and methods. Also, a program with Leadership Education for Asian Pacifics (LEAP) "grows leaders" using simple and powerful tools that include fostering participation in the larger democratic process of business to help APA employees realize their full potential.

 GE invests more than $1 billion a year in the training and professional development of its managers and leaders, engineers, scientists, manufacturing, and sales staff. GE also invites public and private sector leaders to share in this leadership development at GE's Global Learning Centers around the world. The company has a robust slate of programs to develop product leaders of the future and to accelerate the development of an employee's leadership ability so that they are capable of filling and succeeding in more senior, critical roles. With over 200 participants to date, these two to five year programs bring focused efforts to develop high-potential candidates and increase their chances to advance into critical functions in growth markets for GE.

Session C, GE's comprehensive all employee annual review process, includes specific reviews throughout the year where the company identifies APA talent (and other talents) and the type of career broadening experiences they need to reach the next larger role. Those experiences include "stretch" assignments, educations and mentoring. The process identifies high-potential APAs, assesses their current skills and performance, determines management development courses to accelerate their career progression, and assists them with mentor matching and exposure to senior leadership. In addition, the Corporate Diversity Council looks at executive promotions to the C-Suite on a quarterly basis.

The APA employee resource group, APAF, also has programs for the professional development needs of its members. Over the course of 2011, 15 national professional development webinars attracted 3,000+ participants. These programs utilize a wide array of communications technologies to reach more members, provide a library of resources and social networking tools.

Deb Elam, Vice President and Chief Diversity Officer, GE: *"These programs and initiatives are a great way to get people connected, provide a safe environment in which to develop leadership skills. All of this enhances employee confidence and competency in a way to facilitate broader growth."*

One program, the APAF Leadership Development Program, offers quarterly training webinars on relevant topics such as Perspective on 21st Century Leadership, Authenticity, and Transition to Leadership. These webinars are highly popular drawing over 500 registrants for each event. In addition, a targeted initiative focused on APA Women, aims to provide for the professional and personal development needs of this unique group. APAF also held a Talent Development Forum, which provides a platform for high-potential APAs to participate in a year-long program encompassing GE's robust tools of assessment, development, coaching, and career-planning.

Work-Life Effectiveness

All participating companies in the 2012 survey offered a wide array of programs and policies to support their employees in finding work-life balance. These included extensive programs around parental leave, including generous maternity and paternity leave polices and company-specific additions to the federally mandated Family and Medical Leave Act requirements. Child and elder care programs were also widespread. All companies also had provisions and policies for telecommuting and other non-traditional work hours, flexible schedules and sabbaticals, showcasing how these companies are adapting to the needs of today's ever more mobile employees. In fact these programs and policies were so widespread they could be considered standard practice for Fortune 500 level companies. This section specifically highlights other innovative programs that are helping companies better address overall balance in their employees' lives.

Lilly The strength of the work-life programs at **Eli Lilly and Company** is how the company has leveraged the experiences and strengths of its APA employees to foster innovation. This innovation is founded on a culture that supports the employee resource groups at the company level, but remains flexible enough to allow grassroots needs and concerns to be noticed and supported as well. The Chinese Working Mothers Club is one such initiative. The initiative was designed to help the company's Asian ex-patriots and their families integrate into Indianapolis and the Midwest during stints in this country. Recognizing the special challenges of acclimating and acculturating to life in the Midwest, far from traditional centers of Asian and Asian American culture on the coasts, the program relies on the support and expertise of APA employees who host some of these families and provide a source of support and mentoring. To date, the program has add-on networking effects, allowing U.S.-based APA employees to make global connections and vice-versa.

Importantly, the program was aligned with the overall business objective of growing the emerging markets in Asia. The program has been so successful that Lilly is institutionalizing it for other ex-pat groups. In addition, the company's Emerging Markets division is continuing to fund the program as the ex-pat executives return to their home countries with knowledge and connections that will be invaluable as they rise through the ranks and become leaders in the region.

 **KPMG**'s Team of Choice was launched within their Audit practice to teach the client engagement teams to take into account each member's individual work-life priorities and career/skill development goals when planning engagement schedules and deliverables. Through the initiative, teams create customized "Blueprints" that align client expectations with the teams' resources. When developing Blueprints, engagement teams address work-life priorities such as balance and flexibility; skill development; effective staffing and engagement planning; and recognition and appreciation. For example, under work-life balance and flexibility, each team member might choose a day of the week to leave early.

Team of Choice has been so successful as a model that KPMG is starting to see a metamorphosis in a number of ways. It has challenged the perception of what constitutes a team and the accompanying behaviors. There is also widespread recognition that the dynamic workforce is going to perpetually change and the initiative allows for constant evolution. After codifying the learnings from Team of Choice, KPMG is deploying similar initiatives beyond the Audit practice.

CORNING The many work-life balance and effectiveness programs at **Corning** are enhanced by the application of cultural awareness and diversity considerations. For example, managers are given flexibility so that even more junior Asian employees will have sufficient time to go back and visit their families in their home countries, even though their paid time off may not fully cover the longer trips. Corning also goes above and beyond with programs such as its 24/7 teams that respond to the health and safety needs of employees and subsidized child care at the Corning Children's Center, a state of the art facility.

Corning has also made strides in globalizing its work-life and diversity objectives. Grassroots engagement and accountability is very strong within Corning. For example, the activities around Disabilities Awareness Month were celebrated in the U.S., Mexico, Germany and India. In fact, as people with disabilities are a key issue in their country, the Indian office became a sponsor of the Great Delhi Run, helping the organization raise $640,000, the most in its six-year history. This also closely aligned with the opening of a Corning manufacturing facility in India, and allowed the company to establish some name recognition and exhibit its commitment to the community in a very real way.

COLGATE-PALMOLIVE *COMPANY* **Colgate-Palmolive** has developed a global health and wellness sustainability strategy, "Live Better," to inspire people to get engaged and proactively manage their health to improve their personal well-being and that of their families and community. This covers all aspects of "health" from physical to mental to financial etc.

For example, Colgate's Employee Assistance Program assists employees and their families with addressing daily issues they encounter in the workplace and at home, including family issues, physical health, stress and even issues of parenting. The service is strictly confidential and includes legal assistance. A Resource and Referral Program is also offered. The vendor partner's website offers extensive search features, and a variety of interactive tools with content that includes online provider searches and referrals, materials on topics such as Child Care and Parenting, Adult Care and Healthy Aging.

Colgate-Palmolive's financial education program offers three categories of services to help Colgate-Palmolive people better understand and manage their financial life, with individual telephone counseling, a financial planning website, and group workshops. They recently sponsored a financial education program for non-traditional families.

Colgate-Palmolive's employee networks are often integrated into these programs to help spread awareness but to also identify and address issues.

The Global Work Life Council drives **IBM**'s integrated work life strategy, which consists of 3 pillars: Culture, Flexibility and Dependent Care. Extensive programs are developed under each pillar. One such program is the LifeWorks resource and referral program, which helps U.S. employees, and their families handle demands of daily life at work and home through a wide array of innovative features and topics including dependent care. This confidential service, paid for by IBM, is provided by professional consultants who are available 24/7/365 via the toll-free number and on-line access to their website, which houses articles, podcasts, webinars, CDs, booklets, and more. The program also connects employees with a list of providers for needed who are pre-screened to meet IBM's quality standards. In addition, the program supports the decision making process and help employees select the best solution for themselves. The online nature of the program also enables employees to also create virtual online support communities to help manage issues. At times subnets are formed under these larger groups to address other related interests.

Support for the Community

This year's participating companies all had robust programs and relationships with community and grassroots organizations. The highlighted programs showed the most strategic initiatives as evidenced by a wide-ranging array of programs, especially those that were aligned with overall company business objectives. Importantly, while recognition was given to programs in Asia proper, activities focusing on the Asian Pacific American populations were prioritized. In addition, all the Best Practice Companies have struck an important balance between presence at cultural events and business relevant programming with community organizations.

 PG&E continues to reap the benefits of some of the longest standing relationships with APA organizations that effectively reach back to the 1960s. As a utility company, PG&E knows how important it is to continually integrate and understand the communities it serves. PG&E was a founding member of the Corporate Asian American Employee Network (CAAEN) in 2004. CAAEN is a collaborative network of Asian American employee resource groups from the private, public and educational sectors in the Greater Bay Area community. Over the years, the network has grown from the original 12 founding employee groups to over 20 active member organizations, many of which are of Fortune 500 companies. CAAEN is a registered 503(c)3 educational nonprofit.

> Michael Coyle, Principal Program Manager, Diversity & Inclusion, PG&E:
> *"PG&E recognizes that it needs to demonstrate community commitment over and above event sponsorship to provide real and tangible impact to the APA community. This encompasses internal development for employees and our ERG, along with educational development for APA members in our communities along the entire customer life cycle."*

PG&E's activities with annual cultural events such as the Lunar New Year, Tet Festival, Cherry Blossom and Moon Festivals are integrated from a business perspective, with education programs on energy efficiency.

Over the last two decades, InspirAsian, PG&E's employee resource group, also has a robust annual scholarship program that provides scholarships amounting to approximately $30,000 each year to deserving high school seniors. InspirAsian also actively organizes brown bag sessions on referral services for elder care and is an active supporter of Self-Help for the Elderly. Originally created as a "War On Poverty" program, Self-Help for the Elderly began serving seniors in San Francisco's Chinatown community in 1966. Today, Self-Help for the Elderly serves over 25,000 seniors each year in San Francisco, San Mateo, Santa Clara and Alameda counties.

InspirAsian also benefits from a longstanding commitment from senior leadership, along with the longevity of its leadership who has been able to integrate innovation and new ideas into the group's activities.

Goldman Sachs

Goldman Sachs provides significant financial support to a broad array of charitable organizations. However, possibly its greatest contributions come from programs that harness the company's business expertise, relationships and influence to address critical needs in the company's local, national and global communities. For example, in November 2009, Goldman Sachs launched 10,000 Small Businesses, a $500 million investment to help small businesses create jobs and economic opportunity by providing greater access to business education, financial capital, and business support services. The program is based on the broadly held view of leading experts that greater access to this combination of education, capital and support services best addresses barriers to growth.

Another program, 10,000 Women, launched in 2008, is an investment to drive economic growth by providing 10,000 underserved women around the world with a business and management education. The program operates in 22 countries and is coordinated in local markets by a network of more than 80 academic and nonprofit partners. The program has reached more than 5,000 women and nearly 80 percent of surveyed participants have increased revenues and more than 60 percent have added new employees. In March 2011, CEO Lloyd Blankfein, Secretary of State Hillary Clinton and First Lady Michelle Obama announced a new partnership to extend the reach of 10,000 Women and train women entrepreneurs from additional countries around the world, including many Asian countries and the South Pacific islands.

Goldman Sachs Gives is a donor-advised fund (DAF) that the firm established in 2007. Programs include a new partnership with the All China Women's Federation Foundation and

Susan G. Komen for the Cure to positively shift the outcomes of breast cancer education and awareness in China. To coincide with the London 2012 Olympics, a grant of $5 million was split between two organizations, Right to Play and Greenhouse, which each share a vision of the transformative power of sport to change young lives.

Community TeamWorks (CTW) is Goldman Sachs' signature volunteer program started in 1997, which allows Goldman Sachs employees time away from work each year to volunteer on a team-based project with a nonprofit organization. A cornerstone of the culture, CTW's benefit is twofold—it benefits communities and organizations by providing much-needed financial and volunteer support while encouraging teamwork among employees.

Goldman Sachs also sponsors and supports research on the APA workforce, including one of the Center for Work-Life Policy's (CWLP) most recent research reports, "Asians in America: Unleashing the Potential of the Model Minority."

 **KPMG** exemplifies what can be achieved with an extensive network of relationships with APA organizations, as well as those focused on Asia proper. KPMG is a founding sponsor of ASCEND, and was a corporate Platinum Sponsor of the 2011 ASCEND National Conference. Senior members of KPMG are integrally involved in the governance and leadership of the association, including roles as the group's National Treasurer and membership on ASCEND's Board of Directors and Advisory Board. On the local level, many KPMG people serve local ASCEND chapters in capacities such as president, vice president, treasurer, and board member. Most importantly, KPMG has sponsored and participated in numerous programs and workshops at various local ASCEND events. For example, the firm's Washington, D.C./Tysons Corner APIN chapter partnered with the local ASCEND chapter for a "Diversity and the American Workforce" panel discussion. In Houston, the APIN chapter sponsored and hosted ASCEND's "Inspiring Across Generations" conference.

KPMG is also a supporter of the Asia Society and some of the firm's senior executives have important roles on the organization's Corporate Diversity Council and Business Council. KPMG has also been a sponsor of the Asia Society's Diversity Leadership Forum since it was inaugurated.

KPMG's APIN chapters are involved in and support several roundtables that involve members of Asian American employee resource groups representing local companies. For example, KPMG hosted the first meeting that created the New York Asian Affinity roundtable that includes members of prominent organizations.

Through KPMG's local corporate giving program, the firm has supported a variety of Asian-based organizations. During fiscal year 2011, KPMG offices raised funds for a range of Asian Pacific American community organizations, including Asian American Leadership, Baltimore Chinese School, Japan Day, ASCEND, Asia Society, Asian American Federation, China Chamber of Commerce, Chinese American Biomedical Association, Dallas Japan Association, Japan America Society, Japan Club, Japan Society, Japanese American National Museum, Japanese Chamber of Commerce and Industry, JBA Foundation, and The Korea Society.

Lilly's success in supporting the APA community is grounded in its culture of engagement. The company looks for well-rounded individuals who are interested in making a difference inside and outside the company. Just as important is the tone set by the company's overall engagement with the Indianapolis community and the activities of the Lilly Foundation. This translates to a number of health education programs that employees of Lilly are engaged with. In the APA community, Lilly works with key partners such as the Asian American Alliance, Inc. of Indiana that already have well-established links.

Lilly Employees make use of newly installed Walking Treadmill Workstations.

Lilly launches "Get Back on Your Bike" program.

The strongest example of Lilly's support for the APA community is its Clinical Diversity Strategy. Formalized in 2008, the strategy arose from the recognition that to improve individual outcomes, the company needed to ensure that there was a good representation of different human genotypes in its clinical studies, which could result in more tailored, individual treatments. Since testing for genotype is an expensive proposition, race and ethnicity was used as a general, if imperfect, surrogate. Lilly set a goal that for every new trial, at least two sites needed to be classified as clinically diverse, i.e., greater than 25 percent non-Caucasian. The company also endeavored to match the prevalence or incidence of a given disease within a particular race. The company already has 295 diverse sites in 2012. Very few existed in 2008.

 **Freddie Mac** partners with several Asian Pacific American groups to provide homebuyer education and financial literacy to the Asian Pacific American community. The company recognizes the importance and obligation to educate consumers around their product. As part of its overall work helping to stabilize communities and assisting families of every ethnicity to buy and keep their own homes, Freddie Mac developed CreditSmart, a multilingual homebuyer education and financial literacy program. It is designed to help consumers build and maintain better credit, manage their finances, and prepare for successful long-term homeownership. CreditSmart is offered in English, Spanish (CreditSmart Español), and also Chinese, Korean, and Vietnamese (CreditSmart Asian).

CreditSmart Asian, developed with other national Asian Pacific American organizations, is the latest program to help borrowers and potential borrowers within the Asian Pacific American community learn about homeownership today. These organizations then work with their members and affiliates to offer CreditSmart Asian classes to the Vietnamese, Korean, and Chinese immigrant community. Some of these groups include National Coalition for Asian Pacific American Community Development (National CAPACD), NAKASEC, Korean Churches for Community Development (KCCD), AAFE, Asian Real Estate Association of American, Boat People SOS and Chhaya CDC.

Since its official launch on July 26, 2001, approximately 40,000 trained instructors have used CreditSmart to teach more than 3 million Americans in 44 states how to responsibly manage their money, build stronger credit and make wiser financial decisions. In the wake of the current housing and economic crisis, the company realized that its own employees could also benefit from these workshops and have offered them through both on-site and online seminars.

Throughout the year, the company is engaged in many other borrower outreach and consumer education efforts to help prevent foreclosures and promote sustainable home ownership among minority communities across the nation. During the housing crisis, Freddie Mac also provided support to National CAPACD, KCCD, AREAA and Boat People SOS for its foreclosure prevention efforts.

Introducing
The Award Recipients

Introducing the Award Recipients

As part of the 2012 Asian Pacific Americans Corporate Survey, nine companies were recognized for providing inclusive workplaces that promote APAs to corporate leadership positions and draw on APA talent to grow their business at home and abroad. These nine were selected among the finalists for the quality of their APA programs as well as the results from their employee surveys.

Four of the awards are based on a combination of indexed employee scores (80% of total score) as well as scores from the judges (20%). These awards require companies to have participated in both the employee and company portions of the survey.

- ▶ Overall Best Employer for Asian Pacific Americans
- ▶ Best Company for Asian Pacific Americans to Develop Workforce Skills
- ▶ Best Company in Promoting Asian Pacific Americans into Senior Leadership Positions
- ▶ Best Company for Support of the Asian Pacific American Community

In addition, two other awards are given based on the innovation and impact of the programs. Companies can be eligible for these awards by completing the company portion of the survey.

- ▶ Best Company for Mentoring
- ▶ Best Company with the Most Innovative Practices

In addition to the Best Company awards, Honor for Distinguished Practice was also given to one company in each of the categories.

Here are the Award Winners and Distinguished Practice honorees for 2012, including a statement from each winner about their commitment to diversity.

Overall Best Employer for Asian Pacific Americans—KPMG
Diversity and inclusion are strategic priorities for KPMG LLP, and they are woven into everything we do—from recruiting and professional development; the way we serve our clients; our commitment to youth, education, and workforce readiness; and everything in between.

Honor for Distinguished Practice presented to Colgate-Palmolive.

Best Company for Asian Pacific Americans to Develop Workforce Skills—Colgate-Palmolive Company

At Colgate, the rich diversity of our people, our thinking, our talents and our suppliers is vital to our overall success. Maintaining this culture of diversity requires that we live our Values of Caring, Global Teamwork and Continuous Improvement; and that we foster an inclusive work environment in which everyone is encouraged to value one another's unique contributions. Our people are our greatest asset and we are committed to ensuring an environment that celebrates their differences while providing robust opportunities for professional and personal growth in each of the 80 countries where we have operations.

Honor for Distinguished Practice presented to Freddie Mac.

Best Company in Promoting Asian Pacific Americans into Senior Leadership Positions—Freddie Mac

 As a company, Freddie Mac is committed to ensuring an inclusive culture that recognizes and harnesses the diverse interests and contributions of all of our employees. Our ability to attract and retain top, diverse talent and ensure an inclusive work environment is critical to the success of our company and our vital work to serve our mission and support the nation's housing and economic recovery.

Honor for Distinguished Practice presented to Sodexo.

Best Company for Support of the Asian Pacific American Community—New York Life Insurance Company

 At New York Life we proudly recognize our employees' individual attributes and contributions toward making the company such a success. We will continue to seek out and support the best talent, foster a diverse and inclusive culture and maintain an environment in which our employees can thrive. We have no doubt that our support and encouragement of individual differences and unique talents will continue to enhance our business for years to come.

Honor for Distinguished Practice presented to Merck.

The following awards are based entirely on the descriptions of the innovative programs and initiatives that benefit the company's APA employees that were provided to Asia Society on the company portion of the APA Corporate Survey.

Best Company for Mentoring—IBM

THIS AWARD IS NEW FOR 2012.

 For more than a century, IBM has viewed the diversity of cultures, people and ideas as critical to our success in the marketplace. Because our diversity is reflective of the global marketplace, it is integral to our corporate character. And our enduring commitment to diversity is one of the reasons we can credibly say that IBM is one of the world's leading globally integrated enterprises.

Today we also understand that diversity goes beyond fair hiring practices and protection for all employees. It also includes a focus on how those disparate pieces fit together to create an innovative, integrated whole. We call this approach "inclusion." Simply put, it's what we do together that sets us apart.

Honor for Distinguished Practice presented to Corning.

Best Company with the Most Innovative Practices—GE

At GE, diversity is about the power of the mix and the strengths that results from a team with varied experiences, backgrounds and perspectives. Our diversity fosters a limitless source of ideas and opportunities. We are building an inclusive culture, team, environment and processes where diversity is both embraced and leveraged as a competitive advantage in a global marketplace. Diversity is part of our core foundation. From the commitment of our leadership team to our internal processes, inclusiveness energizes teams and fosters teamwork and innovation. Regardless of background, demographics, work style or experience, everyone at GE has an opportunity to contribute and succeed.

Honor for Distinguished Practice presented to IBM.

Asia Society Global Leadership Initiatives

For more than 50 years, Asia Society has been at the forefront of connecting Asians and Americans to foster strong partnerships. In 2011, the Asia Society launched the Global Leadership Initiatives program to identify, develop and inspire leaders across the Asia-Pacific region and to address shared challenges, by convening face-to-face meetings, creating networks, promoting new ideas, and sharing best practices across disciplines.

Asia Society's Global Leadership Initiatives include the: Asia 21 Young Leaders Initiative, Diversity Leadership Forum, Women Leaders of New Asia Initiative and the long-standing Williamsburg Conference, all of which leverage Asia Society's unique role and ability to foster strong Pan-Asian partnerships and leadership across the Asia-Pacific region and different sectors.

ASIA 21 Young Leaders Initiative
AsiaSociety.org/Policy/Asia-21

As the quickening pace of global change presents new challenges that cross national boundaries, Asia and the United States must look to a new generation of leaders for fresh ideas and imaginative solutions. The Asia Society's Asia 21 Young Leaders Initiative is designed to identify, nurture, and develop leaders across the Asia-Pacific community to build relationships, engage in transnational and interdisciplinary dialogue and cultural exchange, and develop cooperative responses for addressing shared challenges. Established in 2006, the Initiative now includes a network of almost 800 young leaders representing every country in the region and all sectors, and has become the Asia-Pacific region's leading network for emerging leaders under the age of 40.

In 2011, an Afghanistan 21 Young Leaders program along with an India-Pakistan Regional Young Leaders program were added to the larger initiative.

Diversity Leadership Forum
AsiaSociety.org/DiversityForum

Established in 2009, the Diversity Leadership Forum provides a vital platform for corporations to discuss diversity and inclusion issues and best practices in regards to Asian professionals and analyze their influence on global market factors impacting businesses today.

The annual one-day conference features:

- ► Ground-breaking research results from Asia Society's annual *Asian Pacific Americans Corporate Survey Report*, a study that examines barriers to and best practices for career advancement of APAs;
- ► Keynote and Plenary Sessions featuring executives from global Fortune 1000 companies;
- ► Small group discussion tracks featuring relevant D&I topics and best practices;
- ► Networking opportunities with organizations and professionals dedicated to the D&I journey; and
- ► Asia Society's 2012 Diversity Awards Ceremony, which recognizes major companies at the forefront of Global Diversity who are Best in Class in Promoting Asian Pacific American Leaders.

The Forum attracts CEOs, CDOs, COOs, Asian Pacific American ERG Leadership and Executive Advisors, Business Managers of Fortune 1000 companies and Diversity and Inclusion Managers, Educators and Consultants.

Williamsburg Conference
AsiaSociety.org/policy-politics/williamsburg-conference

The Williamsburg Conference is the pre-eminent gathering of leading Americans and Asians committed to strengthening U.S.-Asia relations. Founded by John D. Rockefeller, 3rd in 1971, the Williamsburg Conference has brought top leaders from Asia and the United States together to explore the greatest challenges facing the Asia-Pacific community and develop creative approaches for addressing them. In the past 39 years, the conference has been held in the United States, Indonesia, Japan, Hong Kong, Canada, Malaysia, Australia (1977 and 1991), Thailand, the Philippines, Singapore, South Korea, China, Vietnam, New Zealand, India, Cambodia, and Mongolia.

At a time when relations between and among the countries of Asia and the United States are more complicated, and more difficult, than ever before, the Williamsburg Conference seeks to:

► Provide a forum that brings together the top leaders from government, business, academia, and other sectors from across Asia and the United States to thoughtfully explore the most challenging issues facing the Asia-Pacific community and develop proposals for how these challenges can be collaboratively addressed; and

► Build a network of these leaders whose relationships with one another developed through the Williamsburg process can facilitate engaged multi-national and cross-sectoral dialogue and the peaceful resolution of any conflicts that may emerge.

Women Leaders Of New Asia
AsiaSociety.org/WomenLeaders

For more than 50 years, Asia Society has been at the forefront of connecting Asians and Americans to foster strong partnerships in culture, business and global affairs. As women enter the Asian work force in large numbers and step into leadership positions at institutions across the public and private sectors, there is a growing need for new forums to explore the important role of women's leadership in Asia. Few professional networks of Asia-Pacific women currently exist to explore and tackle these issues. To address this gap, Asia Society launched the Women Leaders of New Asia (WLNA) initiative which is fast becoming the premier cross-sector women's leadership network in the Asia-Pacific region.

The Summit fosters discussion around a new paradigm of leadership that recognizes the contribution that women leaders in Asia can make. As Asia's global influence in the political, cultural and economic spheres continues to strengthen, the Summit seeks to explore the new role that women leaders of *"New Asia"* can play.

In 2012, the Asia Society and the Lee Kuan Yew School of Public Policy, National University of Singapore launched: *Rising to The Top? A Report on Women's Leadership in Asia*.

Our Research Partner

proximo Proximo Consulting Services is a services firm that specializes in helping our
consulting.services clients do more with less. Our products and services are used by companies in many verticals to maintain information that is necessary to run their organizations. Proximo has a strong focus on our core competency: data. Everything we do revolves around this. We specialize in data, from the collection and acquisition, to augmenting, and finally to mining, analytics, and business intelligence. Our forte is doing deep dive analytics to answer tough business questions. With this focus, we deliver the best expertise for the best value to our clients.

To have your company participate in the 2013 Asian Pacific Americans Corporate Survey, please contact David Reid at: dreid@AsiaSociety.org.

There is no cost to participate.

Made in the USA
Charleston, SC
22 June 2012